MW00795355

The Souls of Others

ESSAYS

by
Shann Ray

THE SOULS OF OTHERS
Copyright © 2022 Shann Ray
All Rights Reserved.
Published by Unsolicited Press.
Printed in the United States of America.
First Edition.

No part of this book may be used or reproduced in any
manner whatsoever without written permission except in the
case of brief quotations embodied in critical articles or reviews.

Attention schools and businesses: for discounted copies on
large orders, please contact the publisher directly.

For information contact:
Unsolicited Press
Portland, Oregon
www.unsolicitedpress.com
orders@unsolicitedpress.com
619-354-8005

Cover Image: Getty Images
Cover Designer: Kathryn Gerhardt
Editor: S.R. Stewart

ISBN: 978-1-956692-00-6

for Jennifer

CONTENTS

Gratitude bestows reverence, allowing us to encounter everyday epiphanies, those transcendent moments of awe that change forever how we experience life and the world.

—John Milton

Love all of God's creation, the whole and every grain of sand. Love every leaf, every ray of God's light. Love the animals. Love the plants. Love each separate thing. If you love each thing, you will perceive the mystery of God in all. And once you perceive it, you will begin to comprehend it better every day, until you come at last to love the whole world with an all-embracing love.

—Fyodor Dostoevsky

O Lord, remember not only the men and women of goodwill, but also those of ill will. But do not only remember the suffering they have inflicted upon us. Remember the fruits we bought thanks to this suffering—our comradeship, our loyalty, our humility, the courage, the generosity, the greatness of heart which has grown out of this. And when they come to judgment, let all the fruits that we have borne be their forgiveness.

—prayer found crumpled among the remains of the Ravensbrück concentration camp where Nazis exterminated nearly 50,000 women

Like Maps, Like Wisdom Songs:

—Foreword by Joe Wilkins

1.

When I was a boy in Montana I knew beauty in its fullness, a beauty I try again and again to reach back to, to hold once more.

The mountains should be first, the low, broken-backed Bulls, whose boy I was, scouting buttes and box canyons and draws. I'd walk south down Queens Point Road, climb the barbwire fence at the corner post, and set out into the tangle of the Bulls, my own mountain-man stories playing behind my eyes. There were chokecherries to pick, and I'd shear the spines and tough skin from prickly pear cactus and suck the wet inside. I clambered over sandrocks and tossed stones from the cliff, put my lips to the spring's seep and drank deep. I studied greasy gnarls of coyote scat and felt the shadow of an eagle cross me before I ever saw it. Come hunting season, I set my belly to the shadowed earth, just like my grandfather did, and hoped for a buck to come gentle down the game trail below.

Too, there were the Beartooths, the Crazies, the Snowies and Little Snowies—the mountains we decamped to once or twice a summer, the back of the pickup loaded with tents, stoves, fishing rods and tackle boxes, the old green Coleman cooler brimming with beer and strawberry pop. We hiked and threw our lures at the lake and told stories late around the campfire, fishbones popping in the flames. I remember waking to the smell of pine smoke and granite, to mountain mornings so cold my sleeping bag was frosted with my own breath—and still, I couldn't wait to put my hands again in the cold water of the lake.

There were as well the everyday beauties of life on the high plains of Montana. The deep greens and purples of an alfalfa field gone to blossom. Hawks drifting over cottonwoods. A roostertail of dust rising from the gravel road. Another mewling batch of barncats born in the haystack. The noise and light of a small-town gym come Friday night. The slow way my grandmother buttered bread, her voice saying my name. My mother, after my father died, hefting the shovel to go irrigate the place all by herself.

2.

When I was a boy in Montana I knew hunger and loss and the burn in the bones that leads to violence, to dissolution.

Drought and hail and foreclosure notices from the bank, ruinous Western mythologies—all these bore down, kindled despair and even rage. A man quicker with the cattle prod, a woman shorter with a child, a child aiming a kick at the old dog. There were as well the failures that boiled up from the inside, failures of fear and drink and betrayal. And in a place whose deep history was ignored or unacknowledged, in a place where people were spread thin across the land, a place still defined as true frontier, all these forces were only sharpened, clarified.

It's a wonder anyone survives.

My father died when I was nine, and in the years after we struggled to wring any kind of living out of the land. Yet I often thought, and still think, my siblings and I were lucky. My mother was strong and ferocious and did what had to be done. My maternal grandparents lived just a quarter mile down the gravel road, and they were generous with wisdom and laughter and long, meandering conversations after supper. And though my grandparents eventually sold their share of the ranch, and my mother hers, though our losses were manifold, my siblings and I didn't turn mean, didn't succumb to apathy or addiction, didn't get swallowed by the violence that surrounded us.

I don't rightly know how this happened.

In the writing of Shann Ray, though, I begin to see a glimpse.

3.

"Hunger makes us seek, keeps us vital, strikes the soul, makes fire," writes Shann Ray. "I believe our primary hunger is love."

"Montana," Ray writes, "like a microcosm of the country and the world, is also a staging ground for the most fearsome notions of human love and loss."

"The star fields over these mountains," he writes, "lead me home."

In the work of Shann Ray I find the beauty I knew and lost and know now again. I find, too, the hunger and loss and piercing darkness, that which we must admit before we can move on.

And I find what so many of us who call ourselves Westerners (and Americans) are missing: a passionate refusal to look away from violence and atrocity and despair, a passionate refusal, even in the face of the genocidal history of the American West, to give up hope. I find in Shann Ray's essays a soul-igniting belief in history, honesty, wilderness, and forgiveness.

Shann Ray has many teachers, the wing and scope of his vision wide and encompassing. Vincent Van Gogh. Viktor Frankl. Carl Jung. Pierre Teilhard de Chardin. bell hooks. Robbie Paul, professor and direct descendant of Chief Joseph. Emily Dickinson. Czeslaw Milosz. Rilke. Kahlil Gibran. Jim Harrison. Melanie Rae Thon. Debra Magpie Earling. And, too, and even more powerfully, those he calls friends, those he calls family. Cleveland Highwalker. Elvis Old Bull. Jonathan Takes Enemy. Lafe Haugen. Tim Falls Down. Dana Goes Ahead. Blake Walks Nice. Russell Tallwhiteman. Cleveland and Cecelia Bement. His brother. His mother, his father. His three daughters. And most of all, his wife, Jennifer.

I wish as a boy in Montana I could have turned to Shann Ray as one of my teachers, as I do now. I wish I would have been able, all those years ago, to hold these essays—like maps, like wisdom songs—in hand.

I am so thankful I have them now, so thankful you do as well: "We stood not far apart," Shann Ray writes:

our bodies half in water—half dark, half light.

We were alive to each other.

The world was new again.

1.

The Dream

Takes Enemy

Let me enfold thee, and hold thee to my heart.

—Shakespeare, from Macbeth

1

In the dark I still line up the seams of the ball to the form of my fingers. I see the rim, the follow-through, the arm lifted and extended, a pure jumpshot with a clean release and good form. I see the long-range trajectory and the ball on a slow backspin arcing toward the hoop, the net waiting for the swish. A sweet jumper finds the mark, a feeling of completion and the chance to be face to face not with the mundane, but with the holy.

2

In Montana, high school basketball is a thing as strong as family or work and when I grew up Jonathan Takes Enemy, a member of the Crow (Apsaalooké) Nation, was the best basketball player in the State. He led Hardin High, a school with years of losing tradition, into the State spotlight, carrying the team and the community on his shoulders all the way to the State tournament where he averaged 41 points per game. He created legendary moments that decades later are still mentioned in State basketball circles, and he did so with a force that made me both fear and respect him. On the court, nothing was outside the realm of his skill: the jumpshot, the drive, the sweeping left-handed finger roll, the deep fade-away jumper. He could deliver what we all dreamed of, and with a venom that said *don't get in my way.*

I was a year younger than Jonathan, playing for an all-white school in Livingston when our teams met in the divisional tournament and he and the Hardin Bulldogs delivered us a crushing 17-point defeat. At the close of the third quarter with the clock winding down and his team with a comfortable lead, Takes Enemy pulled up from one step in front of half-court and shot a straight, clean jumpshot. Though the range of it was more than 20 feet beyond the three-point line, his form remained pure. The audacity and raw beauty of the shot hushed the crowd. A common knowledge came to everyone: few people can even throw a basketball that far with any accuracy, let alone take a real shot with good form. Takes Enemy landed and as the ball was in the air he turned, no longer watching the flight of the ball, and began to walk back toward his team bench. The buzzer sounded, he put his fist high, the shot swished into the net. The crowd erupted.

In his will even to take such a shot, let alone make it, I was reminded of the surety and brilliance of so many Native American heroes in Montana who had painted the basketball landscape of my boyhood: Jarvis Yellow Robe, Georgie Scalpcane, Joe Pretty Paint, Elias Pretty Horse, the Pretty On Top family. And Cleveland Highwalker, my father's closest friend back then. Many of these young men died due to the violence that surrounded the alcohol and drug traffic on the reservations, but their natural flow on the court inspired me toward the kind of boldness that gives artistry and freedom to any endeavor. Such boldness is akin to passion. For these young men, and for myself at that time, our passion was basketball.

But rather than creating in me my own intrepid response, seeing Takes Enemy only emphasized how little I knew of courage, not just on the basketball court, but in life. Takes Enemy breathed a confidence I lacked, a leadership potential that lived and moved. Robert Greenleaf said, "A mark of leaders, an attribute that puts them in a position to show the way for others, is that they are better than most at pointing the direction." Takes Enemy was better than most. He and his team worked as one as they played with fluidity and abandon. I began to look for this way of life as an athlete and as a person. The search brought me to people who lived life not through dominance but through freedom of movement.

In the half dark of the house, a light burning over my shoulder, I find myself asking who commandeers the vessels of our dreams? I see Jonathan Takes Enemy like a war horse running, fierce and filled with immense power. The question gives me pause to remember him and his artistry, and how he played for something more.

3

Our family was distant. Basketball held us together. As a boy we existed in a nearly rootless way, me and my brother Kral like pale windblown trees in a barren land. Our father's land to be precise, the land of a high school basketball coach.

We were raised in trailers and trailer parks.

My father was a bar fighter.

Getting ready to fight he'd say, "I'm taking my lunch and I'm not closing my eyes."

He meant he wasn't going anywhere. He meant hit hard until it's done.

In college he'd fought his way into the starting line-up, his first two years at Miles City Community College, his final two at Rocky Mountain College. He was a shooter, runner, rebounder, a 6'4 wiry swing man with a smooth outside touch who loved to mix it up on the boards.

After college, he led the family to Alaska and back, then crisscrossed Montana, moving seven times before I was fourteen—all in pursuit of the basketball dynasty, the team that would reach the top with him at the helm and make something happen that would be remembered forever. He'd been trying to accomplish that since before I was born and it got flint hard at times, the rigidity of how he handled things.

4

By the time Kral and I reached high school, we both had the dream, Kral already on his way to the top, me two years younger and trying to learn everything I could. We'd received the dream equally from our father and from the rez, the Crow rez at Plenty Coups, and the Northern Cheyenne (Tsitsistas) rez in the southeast corner of Montana. In Montana tribal basketball is a game of speed and precision passing, a form of controlled wildness that is hard to come by in non-reservation basketball circles. Fast and quick-handed, the rez ballers rise like something elemental, finding each other with sleight of hand stylings and no-look passes, pressing and cutting in streamlike movements that converge to rivers, taking down passing lanes with no will but to create chaos and action and fury, the kind of kindle that smolders and leaps up to set whole crowds aflame.

Kral and I lost the dream late, both having made it to the D-1 level, both with opportunity to play overseas, but neither of us making the league.

Along the way, I helped fulfill our father's tenacious hopes: two state championships at Park High in Livingston, one first as a sophomore with Kral, a massive win in which the final score was 104 to 64, with Kral totaling 46 points, 20 rebounds, and three dunks. And another two years later when I was a senior with a band of runners that averaged nearly ninety points a game. We took the title in what sportswriters still refer to as the greatest game in Montana high school basketball history, a 99-97 double-overtime thriller in 85' at Montana State, the Brick Breeden Fieldhouse, the Max Worthington Arena, before a crowd of 10,000.

Afterward on the bus ride through the mountains I remember my chest pressed to the back of the seat as I stared behind us. The post-game show blared over the speakers, everyone still whooping and hollering. "We're comin' home!" the radio man yelled, "We're coming home!" and from the wide back window I saw a line of cars miles long and lit up, snaking from the flat before Livingston all the way up the pass to Bozeman. The dream of a dream, the

Niitsítapi and the Apsaalooké, the Blackfeet and the Crow, the Néhilawé and the Tsitsistas, the Cree and the Northern Cheyenne, the white boys, the enemies and the friends, and the clean line of basketball walking us out toward skeletal hoops in the dead of winter, the hollow in our eyes lonely but lovely in its way.

5

At Montana State, I played shooting guard on the last team in the league my freshman year. Our team: seven African Americans from across America and five white kids mostly from Montana. We had a marvelous, magical point guard from Portland named Tony Hampton. He was lightning fast with wonderful ball-handling skills and exceptional court vision. He brought us together with seven games left in the season. Our record at the time was 7 wins, 16 losses. Last place in the conference. "We are getting shoved down by this coaching staff," he said, and I remember how the criticism and malice were thick from the coaches. Their jobs were on the line. They'd lost touch with their players. Tony said, "We need to band together right now. No one is going to do it for us. Whenever you see a teammate dogged by a coach, go up and give that teammate love. Tell him good job. Keep it up. We're in this together."

A team talk like that doesn't typically change a season.

This one did.

Tony spoke the words. We followed him and did what he asked, and we went on a seven-game win streak, starting that very night when we beat the 17th ranked team in the country, on the road. The streak didn't end until the NCAA tournament eight games later. In that stretch, Tony averaged 19 points and 11 assists per game. He led the way and we were unfazed by outside degradation. We had our own inner strength. Playing as one, we won the final three games of the regular season. We entered the Big Sky Conference tournament in last place and beat the number fourth, second, and first place teams in the league to advance to March Madness. When we came home from the Conference tournament as champions, it felt like the entire town of Bozeman was at the airport to greet us. We waded through a river of people giving high fives and held a fiery pep rally with speeches and roars of applause. We went on to the NCAA tournament as the last ranked team, the 64th team in a tournament of 64 teams. We were slated to play St. Johns, the number one team in the nation. We faced off in the first game of the southwest regional at Long Beach, and far into the second half we were up by four. St. John's featured future NBA players Mark Jackson (future NBA All-Star), Walter Berry (collegiate player of the year), and Shelton Jones (future winner of the NBA dunk contest). We featured no one with national recognition. We played well and had the lead deep into the second half, up four with eight minutes to go, but in the end, we lost by nine.

When my brother graduated from Montana State I transferred and played my final two seasons of college basketball for Pepperdine University. Our main rival was Loyola Marymount University, featuring consensus All-American Hank Gathers and the multi-talented scorer Bo Kimble. My senior year at Pepperdine we beat Loyola Marymount 127-114 in a true barn-burner! Also a fine grudge match, considering they beat us earlier in the season at their place. We were set to play each other in the championship game of the West Coast Conference tournament but before we could meet at the top of the bracket, Hank died and the tournament was immediately canceled. The tragedy of Hank's death stuns me. He had just completed a thunderous alley-oop dunk and was running back on defense when he collapsed near mid-court and fell, dead of a heart attack. The funeral was in Los Angeles, a ceremony of gut-wrenching grief and bereavement in which we gathered to honor one of the nation's young warriors. We prayed for him and for his family and for all who would come after him bearing his legacy of love for the game, elite athleticism, and the gift of living life to the full. His team went on to the NCAA tournament and made it all the way to the final eight teams, the Elite 8. Bo Kimble shot his first free-throw of the NCAA tournament left-handed in honor of Hank. The shot went in. The nation mourned. The athletes who knew Hank were never the same.

As a freshman in high school, I was tiny, barely five feet tall, and my goal was to play Division 1 basketball. I'd had this goal since I was a child and because of my height and weight it seemed impossible and felt impossible. I was small, but I made a deal with myself to do whatever it might take from my end to try to get to the D-1 level, so if I did not accomplish the goal, I knew at least I had given my all. I grew eight inches the summer before my sophomore year in high school, thanked heaven, and began to think the goal was not totally out of reach.

Hour after hour. Everyday. The dream was now fully formed, bright shining, and excruciating. I played 17 hours in one day. The days of solitude and physical exhaustion were plentiful. I gave my life to the discipline of being a point guard and a shooting guard. I worked on moves, passing, shooting, defending, ball handling. The regimen involved getting up at 7 a.m. at the singlewide trailer we lived in, on my bike by 7:40, traveling downtown in Livingston, yellow transistor radio (borrowed from my mom) in the front pocket of my windbreaker, the ball tucked up under the coat, and me riding to Eastside, the court bordered by a grade school to the east, the Sheriff's station and the firehall to the north, and small residential houses to the west. Eight hours a day my junior summer. Ten hours a day before my senior year. A few blocks south, the Yellowstone River moved and churned and flowed east. Above the river a wall of mountains reached half-way up the sky.

Mostly I was by myself, but because the town had a love for basketball, there were many hours with friends too. In those hours with others, or isolated hours trying to hone my individual basketball skills, I faced many, many frustrations, but finally the body broke into the delight of hard work and found a rhythm, a pattern in which there was the slow advance toward something greater than oneself. Often the threshold of life is a descent into darkness, a powerful and intimate and abiding darkness in which the light finally emerges.

"Beauty will save the world," Dostoevsky said.

Because of basketball I know there exists the reality of being encumbered or full of grace, beset with darkness and or in convergence with light. This interplay echoes the wholly realized vision of exceptional point guards and the daring of pure shooting guards, met with fortitude even under immense pressure.

6

I'm missing the rez, Northern Cheyenne, and I wish I could bring it back, here, now, bring back Lafe Haugen, Russell Tall White Man, Stanford Rides Horse, or Blake Walks Nice with his little side push shot that hits the net in a fast pop because it flies on a straight line, lacking any arc.

After I left the rez, Blake married a Wooden Thigh girl, and they had kids.

Then I heard he was found dead behind Jimtown Bar, stabbed five times in the chest.

7

At Eastside, both low end and high end have square metal backboards marked by quarter-sized holes to keep the wind from knocking the baskets down. Livingston is the fifth windiest city in the world. The playground has a slant to it that makes one basket lower than the other. The low end is nine feet, ten inches high, and we all come here to throw down in the summer. Too small, they say, but we don't listen. Inside-outside, between-the-legs, behind-the-back, cross it up, skip-to-my-lou, fake and go, doesn't matter, any of these lose the defender. Then we rise up and throw down. We rig up a break-away on the rim and because of the way we hang on it in the summer, our hands get thick and tough. We can all dunk now, so the break-away is a necessity, a spring-loaded rim made to handle the power of power-dunks. The break-away rim came into being after Darrel Dawkins, nicknamed Chocolate Thunder, broke two of the big glass backboards in the NBA. On the first one Dawkins' force was so immense the glass caved in and fell out the back of the frame. On the second, the window exploded and everyone ducked their heads and ran to avoid the fractured glass that flew from one end of the court to the other. Within two years every high school in the nation had break-aways, and my friends and I convinced our assistant coach to give us one so we could put it up on the low end at Eastside.

The high end is the shooter's end, made for the pure shooter, a silver ring ten feet, two inches high with a long white net. At night the car lights bring it alive, rim and backboard like an industrial artwork, everything mounted on a steel-grey pole that stems down into the concrete, down deep into the hard soil.

A senior in high school, I'm 17. I leave the car lights on, cut the engine, and grab my basketball from the heat in the passenger foot space. I step out. The air is crisp. The wind carries the cold, dry smell of autumn, and further down, more faint, the smell of roots, the smell of earth. Out over the city, strands of cloud turn grey, then black. When the sun goes down there is a depth of night seemingly unfathomable, and yet the darkness is rent by a flurry of stars.

This is where it begins, the movements and the whisperings that are my dreams. Into the lamplight the shadows strike, separate and sharp, like spirits, like angels. I've practiced here alone so often since Kral left for college I no longer know the hours I've played. I call the ballers by name, the native basketball legends, some my own contemporaries, some who came before. I learn from them and receive the river, their smoothness, their brazenness, like the Yellowstone River seven blocks south, dark and wide, stronger than the city it surrounds, perfect in form where it moves and speaks, bound by night. If I listen my heroes lift me out away from here, fly me farther than they flew themselves. In Montana, young men are Indian and they are white, loving, hating. At Lodge Grass, at Lame Deer, I was afraid at first. But now I see. The speaking and the listening, the welcoming: Tim Falls Down, Marty Round Face and Max and Luke Spotted Bear from Plenty Coups; Joe Pretty Paint from Lodge Grass; and at St. Labre, Juneau Plenty Hawk, Willie Gardner, and Fred and Paul Deputee. All I loved, all I watched with wonder—and few got free.

Most played ball for my father, a few for rival teams. Some I watched as a child, and I loved the uncontrolled nature of their moves. Some I grew up playing against. And some I merely heard of in basketball circles years later, the rumble of their greatness, the stories of games won or lost on last second shots.

8

Falls Down walked with ease in his step, his body loose and free. Tall and lanky, he carried himself with the joy of those who are both loved and strong. He wore his hair tall too. As if guided by wind and light he flew from the ground to the sky, snatched the ball in midair and rocketed an outlet pass to Dana Goes Ahead. He followed his outlet pass, taking a wide arc to the lane where Dana laid down a no look pass and Falls Down finished with a reckless flare, falling to the hardwood as the ball came through the net. I was seven years old. After the game, he spoke to me with humor in his voice and something electric, like lightning.

He was buried at eighteen in buckskin, beads, and full headdress, his varsity uniform, turquoise and orange, laid over his chest: dead at high speed when his truck slid from an ice-bound bridge into the river.

People packed the gymnasium for his funeral.

The old women wailing, their voices ripping a hole in the world.

9

Paul Deputee stood with his chest high, his chin on a level. He looked straight ahead, eyes focused as if on a distant point. His leadership was calm and fast. He took few shots, a selective point guard who always put others before himself. When he chose to shoot, he used a set shot and put a lot of air under the ball. Like water in a cut riverbed his teams followed him without resistance.

Quiet and steady, Paul looked boldly to the future.

He was shot in the head with a high-powered rifle at a party near Crow Agency.

10

Pretty Paint died before he was twenty-five, another alcohol-laced car wreck.

Half-Cheyenne Bobby Jones, dead. A suicide, I believe. By knife or rope or gun, I can't recall.

There are these and many more. "Too many," say the middle-aged warriors, the old Indians, "too young." They motion with their hands as if they pull from a bottle. With their lips they gesture and place their index finger and thumb to their lips in a mock image of dope. They spit on the ground. Some of those who died held me in their hands when I was a boy, when they were young men. I remember their faces, their hair like a black wing, eyes the push of mountains, silvery laughter ever-present in their smile.

Of the living and the dead, two above the rest: Elvis Old Bull and Jonathan Takes Enemy. Stars I played with and against. Both Crow. Elvis was three-time M.V.P. of the State tournament: ambidextrous, master passer, prolific point maker. And Takes Enemy scored like none other. He shot the leather off the ball.

The Crow reservation runs the Montana-Wyoming border in a place of plateau flatlands. The carved canyon of the Bighorn River like a vein on the land. A haze of mountains at the edge of the eye. Top a grassy rise and make a slight descent to the Little Bighorn battle site, the Battle of the Greasy Grass, where Lakota, Cheyenne, and Arapaho (Hinono'eiteen) forces took Custer and kissed the earth with his blood. Crow Agency is the centerpiece, the town like a tangled chessboard made of sticks and gravel, frayed to open fields. Out there, horses stand in twos and threes, windblown and slope-backed. Lodge Grass, a smaller outpost further south.

Old Bull, long-legged with a slender barrel-chest, like a fluted wine glass. When he was a few years out of high school and I'd finished college we played a money tournament together in northeast Montana. Three grand in prize money for the champions. To raise money for the local high school, on Friday night the small white town gathered and auctioned off the shooters for Saturday's three-point contest. Elvis Old Bull's jumper went for a couple thousand dollars to an old rancher, and Elvis made good on the investment. In the championship game on Sunday against a group comprised of wingmen slashers and a few guards from the Canadian National Team, we rode to victory on the back of Old Bull's exquisite passing. He threw assist after assist, dime after dime, opening wide the dunk lanes to the delight of a crowd made mostly farmers and ranchers, their wives, and children. In the second half the crowd raised the roof after a shot Old Bull made that still stands like a torch in my memory. He crossed half-court hounded by defenders, a spin move once at the hash mark, another at the top of the key where he went directly into his jumpshot. But when he spun, the defender was draped on his shooting hand. In midair, nonchalant, Elvis switched the ball position and shot left-handed, holding his follow through with gorgeous form even with his off hand.

All net.

Applause and shouts of praise from the crowd.

Elvis smiling on an easy backpedal down court.

Year by year, I saw less of him.

He grew large, heavy-headed with alcohol.

Much later I met his son at a tournament in Billings. I didn't see Elvis and haven't seen him since.

11

27 feet. 30. The NBA line is 23 feet, nine inches. The message is an echo in my mind, only one shot at the game-winner. In the 99-97 double-overtime title game my senior year in high school our team rallied, my friend John Moran hit two game-sealing free throws and we won in the closing seconds, the gym-noise like an inferno. My brother met me and we stayed up all night and laughed together and talked hoops.

12

The body in unison, the step, the gather, the arc of the ball in the air like a crescent moon—the follow-through a small well-lit cathedral, the correct push and the floppy wrist, the proper backspin, the arm held high, the night, the ball, the basket, everything illumined.

We are given moments like these, to rise with Highwalker and Falls Down and Spotted Bear, with Round Face and Old Bull and Takes Enemy: to shoot the jumpshot and feel the follow through that lifts and finds a path in the air, the sound, the sweetness of the ball on a solitary arc in darkness as the ball falls into the net.

All is complete. The maze lies open, an imprint that reminds me of the Highline, the Blackfeet and Charlie Calf Robe, the Crow and Joe Pretty Paint, a form of forms that is a memory trace and the weaving of a line begun by Indian men, by white men, by my father and Calf Robe's and Pretty Paint's fathers, by our fathers' fathers, and by all the fathers that have gone before, some of them distant and many gone, all of them beautiful in their way.

13

The moon is hidden, the sky off-white, a far ceiling of cloud lit by the lights of the city. Snow falls steady and smooth like white flowers. I put the ball down and blow in my hands to warm them. My body is limber, my joints loose. I have a good sweat going. It's just my hands that need warming so I eye the rim while I blow heat into them. The motion comes to me, the readying, the line of the ball, the line of the sky. I remove my sweat top and throw it out in the snow toward the car. I'm in a grey t-shirt. Steam lifts from my forearms.

Oceans and continents away from home, pro ball in Germany, in an old small gym in Düsseldorf, four seconds on the clock and the team down 1, I missed the free-throw we needed to get to the playoffs.

Growing up I missed my father. We missed each other.

The Blackfeet reservation is in the far northwest corner of the State, tucked against two borders. Glacier National Park to the west, to the north Canada. Bearhat and Gunsight and Rising Wolf Mountains. The Great Garden Wall. The Marias and Two Medicine Rivers. The backbone of the continent. Browning is a lean spread of buildings on the windswept steppe below the great rocks. Thin rail line near black in the dark. Amtrak's Empire Builder like a shout on the outskirts of town.

Fresh from professional ball in Germany I went with my dad to the Charlie Calf Robe Memorial Tournament on the Blackfeet rez. The tribe devoted an entire halftime to my father and he didn't even coach on that reservation. They presented him with a beaded belt buckle and a blanket for the coaching he'd done on other reservations—to show their respect for him as an elder who was a friend to the Native American tribes of Montana. During the ceremony they wrapped the blanket around his shoulders, signifying he would always be welcome in the tribe.

On that weekend with him, I received an unforeseen and wholly unique gift. Dedicated as a memorial to the high school athlete Charlie Calf Robe, a young Blackfeet artist, long distance runner, and basketball player who died too early, the tournament was a form of community grieving over the loss of a beloved son. The Most Valuable Player (MVP) award was made by Charlie's wife, Honey Davis, who spent nine months crafting an entirely beaded basketball for the event. When the tribe and Honey herself presented the ball to me, and I walked through the gym with my father, an old Blackfeet man approached us. He touched my arm and smiled a wide smile.

"You can't dribble that one, sonny" he said.

14

Marty Round Face was smooth and fast. He ran strong and flew high. When he cut to the middle and parted the

34

defenders he rose like something celestial and let the ball fall off his fingers into the net, echoing the Iceman, George Gervin, of the San Antonio Spurs. As a boy, when I watched him my heart filled with expectation.

"How does he jump so high?" I asked my father.

"He works at it," my father said. "He cut a lodge pole and stuck it in the field behind his house. He placed small pieces of yarn up high on the pole, each one six inches above the other. That's how he leaps, son. Practices day after day until he reaches the next piece of yarn."

Marty Round Face leapt to touch the sun.

The entire town flocked to see him.

Not long after high school he committed suicide.

15

Young, I spent much of my life lost in loneliness and fear. My father, as I grew to know and love him, may have been lonelier still.

I saw my father's father only a handful of times.

He lived in little more than a one room shack in Circle, Montana. In the shack next door was my grandfather's brother, a trapper who dried animal hides on boards and leaned them against walls and tables. I remember rattlesnake rattles in a small pile on the surface of a wooden three-legged stool. A hunting knife with a horn handle. On the floor, small and medium-sized closed steel traps. An old rifle in the corner near the door.

My father and I drive the two-lane highway as we enter town. We pick up my grandfather stumbling drunk down the middle of the road and take him home.

Years later my grandpa sits in the same worn linoleum kitchen in an old metal chair with vinyl backing. Dim light from the window. His legs crossed, a rolled cigarette lit in his left hand, he runs his right hand through a shock of silver hair atop his head, bangs yellowed by nicotine. Bent or upright or sideways, empty beer cans litter the floor.

"Who is it?" he says, squinting into the dark.

"Tommy," my dad says, "your son."

"Who?" the old man says.

When we leave, my grandpa still doesn't recognize him.

On the way home through the dark, I watch my father's eyes.

My grandfather was largely isolated late in life. No family members were near him when he died. He once loved to walk the hills after the spring runoff in search of arrowheads with his family. But in my grandpa's condition before death his desire for life was eclipsed. He became morose and very depressed. In the end, alcohol killed him.

16

One shot. The ball is perfect, round and smooth. The leather conforms to my hands. I square my feet and shoulders to the rim and let the gathering run its course. At the height of the release my elbow straightens. I land, and my hand as it follows through is loose and free, the ball the radiant circle I've envisioned from the moment I looked out the trailer window, even now in sheer darkness a small sphere in orbit to the sun that is my follow through, a new world risen with its own glory here among the other worlds, the playground, the schoolhouse, the Sheriff's station, the firehall.

The Cheyenne rez abuts the Crow rez but moves further east. The Powder and Tongue Rivers run through a dry land of flats and coulees, sandstone ridges and scrub pine. The main town, Lame Deer, is set at the juncture of a crossroads among low hills. Dirt side streets and makeshift cul-de-sacs, clusters of pastel colored HUD houses. Jimtown Bar is just past the north rez line, a neon flash on the highway before the big industrial smokestacks of the Montana Power Company in Colstrip.

When young, my father drove the backroads of that rez with Cleveland Highwalker. The two were inseparable. Town ball and tournaments, laughter and brotherhood. I remember my dad's hand on my jaw, gently. Him telling me how he went with Cleveland into the far hills in winter to make a trade with Cleveland's grandmother for two sets of beaded moccasins. Him punching through snow to bring two deer, a gopher, and a magpie to the old Highwalker woman who spoke only Cheyenne and traced his footprints on leather she later chewed to soften. The picture of it makes me wonder now if there is still blood for forgiveness. Dead things for the new day.

"Cleveland was flat-out an athlete," my dad said. "And he could sky. Leap straight out of the gym."

My father shakes his head. Water in his eyes. "Wouldn't find a better player anywhere, and no better friend."

Not long after high school, married and on the way to fatherhood, Cleveland took his own life.

At the funeral, the small box church overflowed.

People lined up outside and looked in through the open windows.

17

My cousin Jacine, a beautiful young woman, fell headlong into drug culture.

She died of multiple bullet wounds in a drug shootout on the south end of Billings near Montana Avenue. I think of my aunt in Montana. Our family, still mourning.

I think of Takes Enemy and Walks Nice. Joe Pretty Paint's father, his generations, his country overcome by violent men. I think of his mother loss, and father loss. And my father and mother, their sisters and brothers ... the losses that reside in our blood like shards of glass.

18

In present-day Montana, with its cold winters and far distant towns, the love of high school basketball is a time-honored tradition. Native American teams have most often dominated the basketball landscape, winning multiple state titles on the shoulders of modern-day warriors who are both highly skilled and intrepid.

Tribal basketball comes like a fresh wind to change the climate of the reservation from downtrodden to celebrational. Plenty Coups with Luke Spotted Bear won two state championships in the early eighties. After that, Lodge Grass, under Elvis Old Bull won three straight. Jonathan Takes Enemy remains perhaps the most revered. Deep finger rolls with either hand, his jumpshot a thing of beauty, with his quick vertical leap he threw down 360s, and with power. We played against each other numerous times in high school, his teams still spoken of by the old guard, a competition fiery and glorious, and then we went our separate ways.

For a few months he attended Sheridan Community College in Wyoming then dropped out.

He played city league, his name appearing in the Billings papers with him scoring over 60 on occasion, and once 73.

Later I heard he'd done some drinking, gained weight, and become mostly immobile.

But soon after that he cleaned up, lost weight, earned a scholarship at Rocky Mountain College and formed a nice career averaging a bundle of assists and over 20 points a game.

A few years ago, we sat down again at a tournament called the Big Sky Games. We didn't talk much about the past. He'd been off the Crow reservation for a while, living on the Yakima reservation in Washington now. He said he felt he had to leave to stay sober. He'd found a good job. His vision was on his family. The way his eyes lit up when he spoke of his daughter was a clear reflection of his life, a man willing to sacrifice to enrich others. His face was full of promise and thinking of her he smiled. "She'll graduate from high school this year," he said, and it became apparent to me that the happiness he felt was greater than all the fame that came of the personal honors he had attained.

Jonathan Takes Enemy navigated the personal terrain necessary to be present for his daughter. I hope to follow him and be present for my daughters. By walking into and through the night he eventually left the dark behind and found light rising to greet him.

19

Inside me are the memories of players I knew as a boy, the stories of basketball legends. The geography of such stories still shapes the way I speak or grow quiet, and shapes my understanding of things that begin in fine lines and continue until all the lines are gathered and woven to a greater image. That image, circular, airborne, is the outline and the body of my hope.

Even now, at over 50 years old, in the evening the drive is not far and before long I take the ball from the space in the backseat of my car and walk out onto the court. I approach the top of the key where I bounce the ball twice before I gather and release a high-arcing jumpshot.

Beside me, Blake Walks Nice sends his jumper into the air and Joe Pretty Paint's follow through stands like the neck of a swan.

The ball falls from the sky toward the open rim. The sound is a welcome sound.

I breathe and stare at the net, at the ball that comes to rest in the key.

Behind us and to the side only darkness.

An arm of steel extends from the high corner of the building in the schoolyard.

A light burns there.

The Art of Basketball, Writing, and Good Smack Talk:

Shann Ray and Jess Walter in Conversation at Tin House

Tin House editorial note: *As the NBA season kicks off this evening, we decided to ask two of our favorite literary hoopers to drop a few dimes for us. As they are prone to do, Shann and Jess sprinkled the court with beautiful jumpers that covered a wide range of topics including faith in writing.*

I met Jess Walter in 2004 over basketball and words, and the friendship formed has been a beauty. Jess is one of those writers who gives uniquely and fully to the community, and it's tangible and refreshing how the community has such genuine affection not just for his work, but for him and his family. His novels, stories, and nonfiction meet us where we are and surprise us, informing us of things we didn't know about ourselves but needed to know, and things we knew but perhaps were afraid to consider more closely. Add to this the fact that he's a true hooper. He has a gorgeous rainbow jumper. He's a wonderful teammate who goes all out every time he plays: scoring, passing, and defending "with alacrity" (in the words of my favorite basketball announcer Bill Raftery). And as you'll see below, he can talk smack, be it material or meta-physical, with the best of them. —Shann Ray

Shann Ray: Let's start with some basketball junkie material. What's your favorite shot on the court?

Jess Walter: My favorite shot is one that you've mastered—no passes, just the ball handler pulling up way beyond the 3-point line (with you, just over half-court.) Bringing the ball down, pulling up and draining a three is the equivalent of a slam dunk. Demoralizing. Nothing anyone can do and it causes the other player to just drop his arms. It's an ace in tennis, a kickoff return in football, a knockdown in boxing. As an opposing point guard once said to me as he pulled up for one of those, my arms at my sides, knees buckled, "Read it in the paper, baby."

I'd love to know about the places in Montana where you lived, and whether, growing up there, you were aware of the things you write about, the awful injustice perpetrated against tribes, the long shadows of the mining industry. I would also be curious if there are books that, for you, manage to get the interior West right. I think we both admire James Welch's *Fools Crow* more than just about anything. I thought Denis Johnson's *Train Dreams* was great and spare, too. What else do you find yourself returning to? First, your favorite shot though.

SR: I appreciate the deep fade away from the corner with a couple of defenders draped on you. Something so fulfilling about the ball on a strange high arc from nearly behind the backboard on a far baseline angle, with an all net finish. I've seen your rainbow J hit pure net from there, my friend! It's a crowd pleaser. A rainmaker. And the sound of the ball in the net seems somehow amplified. But that might be just in my head. I recall the all-state player Joe Pretty Paint from the Crow rez in southeast Montana bombing those threes like he was shooting from the lobby. His follow through was luminous, like the neck of a swan. Oh, and good trash talk is a thing of beauty too. One of the favorite lines another player used on me after he put his jumper in my eye: "Got him, Coach."

I grew up all over Montana, born in Billings, then moved to Sitka, Alaska for six years, then back to Montana, to Bozeman, then Billings again where my dad coached basketball on the nearby Crow reservation, then we moved to the Northern Cheyenne reservation where I went to middle school (so much good basketball–the passing, shooting, and fast break speed impressed me so much and formed my game for years to come). After that, Livingston, between the Crazies and the Beartooths, huge mountain ranges with rivers like mercury.

I didn't know of the genocidal tendencies of America at that time. I could, however, feel the deep tension between dominant culture and non-dominant culture. I knew nothing of the grave harms against humanity, committed by U.S. military against the Cheyenne. In fact, Cheyenne people gave so much love to me and my family when I lived on the reservation, it humbled me and shaped me into a better human being. The gift culture, circular and full of quick wit and near constant humor, so counter and subversive in its way, made me question the rigid linear way

I'd perceived the world around me before living there. The shadow of America, that unspoken history of colonization, revealed deep wounds: high unemployment, rampant addiction, and a certain oblique grief like a pall over everyone. But in the midst of this, I encountered affection and love, a love that will always be with me, given by friends Lafe Haugen, Russell Tall Whiteman, Cleveland Bement, and Blake Walks Nice.

The writing I return to comes from the heart of Montana: James Welch (*Winter in the Blood* and *Fools Crow*), Sandra Alcosser (*Except by Nature*), Ivan Doig (*This House of Sky*), Melissa Kwasny (*Thistle* and *Reading Novalis in Montana*), Wallace Stegner (his collected stories), M.L. Smoker (*Another Attempt at Rescue* and her anthology of human rights poems edited with Melissa Kwasny, *I Go to the Ruined Place*), Richard Ford (*Wildlife* and *Rock Springs*, not the later books), A.B. Guthrie's *The Big Sky*, Richard Hugo's *Triggering Town*, and Annick Smith's *Homestead*. I cherish *Train Dreams* too, along with *Jesus' Son* and *Tree of Smoke*.

Tell me, whose game do you like the most in the NBA right now? And after that, I find in your books something like the sting of American capitalism gone awry next to the emotional capacity for a love that still shocks us and makes us whole, even as things disintegrate around us. How do you do that? What gnaws at you to craft these people who make us yearn for so much, and who make us hope again even when our capacity for hope is less than robust?

JW: That NBA question is interesting, Shann. I played basketball as a kid because, unlike football, the other huge sport at the time, basketball seemed like it was about grace and athleticism rather than sheer brute force (of which I had none). But basketball is, clearly, also about force. There are players looking for space and players looking for contact. I'm a space guy. So, for me, Steph Curry and Klay Thompson are the most thrilling players to watch because they glide around the court looking for the tiniest bit of space for their perfect jumpers. But LeBron James has the athleticism and brute force. He'll drive right into a player's chest or use his huge shoulders to create that space. It's fascinating to watch the NFL and the NBA continuously alter their rules to make their games less violent, to give grace a chance against brute force. Because we know what wins in the end.

And you? Probably few of your readers know that you were a terrific college basketball player at Montana State and Pepperdine and pro ball in Germany's top league, the Bundesliga—and that you've continued to play exhibitions and pickup games against the best players in the country. Whose NBA game do you admire? And who is the best player you ever scored on? (not including me)

Also, I suppose I write inside-out—create characters with as much specificity as I can and then put them in the world they might know, so if they bang against walls of capitalism, authority or society, it is through the endless loop of a bank's computerized phone system, or a pawn shop that no longer has use for 3-year-old, $2,000 television. I think it's fascinating, and audacious, that you often go for the full scope and sweep of the worlds you're creating—the first image you paint in *American Copper* is of miners going into the earth, "where no man belonged," immediately creating a voice that exists above, a voice that can descend on a family with "more money than the Montana state treasury" or the heart-rending massacre of a Cheyenne village. I imagine you seeing your landscapes almost like a painter does (or like the poet you are) ... do you sense that you work outside-in?

You also move seamlessly through time. There's a famous saying (its origin is foggy)—"The past is another country. They do things differently there." But I wonder if that is less true in the literature of the West. Is it just the relative youth of the Western United States that makes us more connected to its past? Or do we still do things the same way?

SR: I love that idea, Jess... giving grace (and space) a chance against brute force. It speaks to me of elegance of movement, elegance of thought. My favorite players have a nearly unconscious foresight in which they make the imaginative move, and finish with beauty in the midst of brute force. Like you, Steph Curry is one I love to watch, and with him, equally as devastating in accuracy and grace, Kevin Durant. I'm in awe of how both of them, one near 7 feet tall, the other closer to 6 feet, have such similar understandings of meta-rhythm as they play, passing, shooting, defending and scoring with such grace and ease. I could watch them work all day. I also admire their surprising sense of humility, their love for family and community. Perhaps strange for high level stars, and certainly refreshing.

I, on the other hand, am a braggart! What a word. I cherish the give and take friendship-based trash talk in basketball, the underlying respect it entails, and the way it gives a community of ballers joy. There's rude/mean/low trash talk, and there's just good quality friendship/humor trash talk. I subscribe to the latter and practice it near constantly. I'm delighted when others trash me back. Like when you talked about my mom the other day... something about you taking her to school. I'm pretty sure she took you to school in reality though. Of those I've scored on, most are from the distant past: Penny Hardaway, Jamal Mashburn, Bobby Hurley, Grant Hill (had 22 at Duke's Cameron Indoor with one two-handed smash), Stacy Augmon and Greg Anthony at UNLV (those two were the filthiest trash talkers around, but gave me a nod of respect when I tried to throw down on Moses Scurry and got fouled), and Baron Davis (28 against UCLA at Pauley Pavilion), but generally they all worked me over and their teams always won more than mine did.

The outside in or inside out I hadn't considered until you mentioned it; that conceptualization and visioning work we go through. I envision a kind of beauty below all, below the paradox and mystery of human existence, below the evil we do to one another and the existence of uncommon good, below the binary rigidity and the fracturing, and below the simple kindness. I think of this beauty as love, and it reminds me of Calvin's notion that perhaps each of us has 1,000 angels walking with us, trying to help us find our way, and that their sorrow is sometimes felt raking the earth. I think of it as captured in Hopkins' desolate sonnets and also his poems of ecstasy... the inscape of sprung lines he utters in his own hard depression and despite the world's industrial raping of Nature... "The world is charged with the glory of God." I think engaging our doubts with courage is a grave responsibility, and though I have no full affirmation of what faith is... I hope for it. I hope in us, in the notion of beloved things, people, existence… of a beloved. My wife and three daughters embody this to me.

As for the past, in the West, and around the globe, I think we forget too quickly, and I believe remembering is a kind of grieving we need in order to lean more fully into atonement. Remembering and grieving together, toward atonement. The return to oneness. At-one-ment. Remembering the past, in the present, toward the future. My research into forgiveness and reconciliation worldwide has been a shattering journey of the last 25 years, and one in which I feel art is renewed and made more musical, more harmonic: I think of Morrison, Milosz, Lorca, Silko, George Elliott, Erdrich, Coetzee, Berger, Li-Young Lee, the painter Makoto Fujimura… back to your idea of making room for grace against brute force.

And what is grace, in art, in life, and in basketball? Does grace exist through its unity with grit? What is it about something pure or close to pure in life and basketball that attracts us? What is chemistry, how do artists and athletes gain that place of real chemistry/connection resulting in something transcendent between writer and reader, between an athlete and her or his teammates? What's your experience of it? I hope I'm not projecting some false assumption, but I hear it like a clarion call in your stunning collection of short stories *We Live in Water* and in the deep painful echo of our shared humanity in *The Zero, The Financial Lives of the Poets,* and *Beautiful Ruins.*

JW: Shann, that is an amazing all-star team you've played against! It does strike me as odd that you didn't put my name in there, but I'm guessing that was just an oversight. It says something about your abilities, too, that you might be the best player I've scored against. And dude, I have OWNED you. Well, maybe not owned, but I do recall a little floater that caused you to shake your head once. I also stuck a couple of jumpers in Richie Frahm's eye one summer when he was home from playing in the NBA, but I have to think he was going about half speed since he was wearing loafers.

And you are NOT a braggart. You show great humility. If I had played against those guys, I'd begin every sentence with, "The time I took Stacy Augmon off the dribble …" However, you DO talk your share of smack, as anyone who has played against you will attest. I've never been a smack talker. I prefer to let my air balls and turnovers do my talking for me.

I also loved that smooth connection you made between gracefulness in sports and the idea of grace in humanity (and in poetry, short stories, essays, and novels). It was a sweet rhetorical crossover dribble, from one meaning of grace— fluid, elegant movement, Durant and Curry—to the other— the idea of favor and forgiveness bestowed upon humanity (or aspired to by humanity), a blessing, an earned peace. I always hitch on this kind of grace though, because of the implication that something has bestowed the grace, in the religious sense, as in a supreme being.

Also, great and thought-provoking was your question, "Does grace exist through its unity with grit?" (There's no grace left in my basketball game, it's all the grit in my knees where the cartilage used to exist.) But my view of the world, yes—I do like to think that hard work and humility lead to this quality of grace, that the meek shall indeed inherit …

well, if not the whole earth, at least the 46 percent of it that the 1 percent isn't using to play tennis.

But my agnostic inclination is to break your question in half: "Does grace exist?" As I said, I always find myself not quite tracking that second meaning of grace, like a defender who hasn't quite kept up with the ankle-breaking crossover. Of course people act with something we might call grace. They seek something we might identify as grace (or another great word you used, atonement.) I think, as a writer, especially in *We Live in Water*, this is what I'm exploring: the characters' capacity for finding this quality in themselves and others. I often think in terms of the word redemption, and I wonder if my little characters can make significant changes in their lives or if they are like the fish in the aquarium in the title story, constrained by patterns and limits they don't even see. It's something you explore beautifully in your writing, and often from terrific vantages. You seem drawn to historical darkness and to violence. I almost imagine you seeking out this quality like a deep-sea diver intent on discovering life existing even at the darkest depths.

But I wonder if there isn't a big distinction in the way we are imagining this thing we are calling grace, and if this doesn't go back to my earlier idea of inside/outside. You describe this quality of grace, this beauty, as existing "below all, below the paradox and mystery of human existence ..."

That's such a lovely idea, but the empiricist in me suspects that grace is not a free-floating state of being but a construct of society and language (as is "the paradox and mystery of human existence.") Not to get too far down the philosophical rabbit hole, but to me, the mystery of feline existence doesn't exist until the cat contemplates it. And my cat usually just seems to be contemplating his own ass. Now I don't think I'm a complete logical positivist (believing that meaning can only be ascribed to those things that can be empirically measured) but the satirist in me, the ironist, can't really see how grace or beauty or love, as much as I hold these concepts above all the others, would have more inherent meaning than those other things whose existence are proven by the mere fact that humans believe they have "experienced" them: superstition, fear, grandiosity, psychosis, delusion (but also humor and pride and happiness.)

But enough of my amateur philosophizing: this is what I've always loved about our conversations—playing basketball and then grabbing a hamburger and six Mountain Dews (five of them yours) and debating the nature of grace! And I also find it interesting that our two different approaches might arrive at similar places. We generally value the same things—families and friends, basketball and literature. We both have a powerful sense of social justice and I imagine we would almost always agree on what is the right course, that we generally have arrived at a similar answer to Montaigne's challenge that philosophy be used to determine "the way to live." So there's some smack talk to end with—Montaigne: "Nothing is so firmly believed as that which we least know." Read in the paper, baby!

SR: For the audience, did anyone notice how Jess said, "I've never been a trash talker." Then he followed it up with a litany of smack. I like that, how trash is always laced with a disruptive and often hilarious undertone. Not only that, but he also took his smack to a new level, talking metaphysical trash! Game on, my friend. By the way, Mountain Dew is the nectar of God.

I take a little pride in the fact that the country of my grandmother's heritage, Czechoslovakia, somehow generated the Velvet Revolution which helped bring about the end of oppressive communism in that country, without bloodshed. Then they elected Vaclav Havel, a playwright, a writer no less, as the president of their new democracy. They turned from logical positivism, from the world's number one experiment in atheistic materialism, back to more mystic forms of humility in the face of the collective, in the presence of the Divine. Havel stated in his essay The Power of the Powerless:

> "Consciousness precedes Being, and not the other way around, as Marxists claim. For this reason, the salvation of this human world lies nowhere else than in the human heart, in the human power to reflect, in human modesty, and in human responsibility. Without a global revolution in the sphere of human consciousness, nothing will change for the better."

This begs the questions: what is salvation? and who guides the human heart? Like Havel, and his precursors Masaryk, Patocka, and Husserl, I find it too self-embedded to think we solely guide ourselves, and too elusive or irresponsible to say only forces beyond us guide our lives. In the Czech lands the martyrdom of Jan Hus, mirrored by the self-immolation of Jan Palach following the Soviet truncation of the Prague Spring, forms an important part of this dynamic. What makes sense to me, having encountered love, is that we are anchored by Love and we have responsibility to give Divine love to one another, our individual and collective being anchored to greater Being which is the morality that destines us toward compassion when faced with the evil we find ourselves capable of at every turn. Back to what to do with our own evil? I believe the Divine helps us ask that question and calls us to discern our response to life.

Having been trained in the logical positivist worldview as a social science quantitative researcher (in the tradition of Locke and Newton), and also trained in the circular interpretivist worldview of the phenomenologists as a social science qualitative researcher (Gadamer, Heidegger, Husserl, Merleau-Ponty, Ricouer, and Levinas, and add in Foucault on power even with his violent rejection of the phenomenologists), the process is humbling. The benefit of both becomes readily apparent, of not carving out a binary but replacing it with a holistic sense of these two ways of viewing the world through human science, of looking at understanding life, having wisdom, or seeking what's real or what's true. Forgiveness research from an empirical positivist quantitative stance shows evidence of higher forgiveness capacity being significantly related to lower anxiety, anger, and depression, as well as significant correlations between forgiveness and less heart disease. For me, that evidence points to the Divine in everyday life and the Divine below, within, and beyond us. Forgiveness research from an empirical interpretivist qualitative stance shows the essence of forgiveness makes a new bridge between people, a bridge made of modesty, surrender, vulnerability, strength, and courage. Again, for me, that points to the interwoven chord of the human and the Divine.

Of course human history is replete with human evil, often cloaked in religion (religion of all forms). All major religions have directly violated people en masse. Christianity, Islam, Confucianism, even Buddhism. Blaming this on God is too weak intellectually, I believe. In the name of material positivism, atheism, and empirical "science," the same gross violations against humanity have occurred (Mao, Stalin, Hitler; Eugenics; the Nuclear Age, etc.). I think the blame should be placed on our own ill conceptions of God or anti-God and our ill conceptions of each other. I believe the Divine, or God, Maheo of the Northern Cheyenne, shrouded in mystery, exists below all, beyond all our conceptions, and is inherently good, or life-seeking. Counter to death, entropy, and closed systems.

Talk about longwinded. Sorry. Okay, I swallowed up the air space there for a minute. Back to trash talking. I agree with you, a hard-won agnosticism, or a hard-won atheism is similar in many ways to a hard-won belief on the doubt/faith continuum. I know you and I both doubt. We both believe in healthy skepticism, and we know that we can never really know. We both arrive at social justice, a love for humanity, and a belief in our responsibility to live responsible lives. It's the facile, unconscious life as well as the unprincipled life that we hope to transcend in ourselves and in our writing. I love that about our conversations too. Your view of life influences me on the deepest levels.

That deep dive into human darkness is common to us both as writers. I find your sensibility gorgeous, deft, and something that blooms like the wildflowers of Montana from that high alpine soil. Something close to the sun.

That said, I'll close with some words from the French Jesuit philosopher-poet and renowned scientist Pierre Teilhard de Chardin. First, this passage that describes our friendship, for which you have my gratitude: "There is almost a sensual longing for communion with others who have a large vision. The immense fulfillment of the friendship between those engaged in furthering the evolution of consciousness has a quality impossible to describe." And second, more from Teilhard de Chardin, now toward the metaphysical forming us to see beyond the over-focus on "mastering the material" that I believe envelopes the Western world: "Someday, after mastering the winds, the waves, the tides and gravity, we shall harness for God the energies of love, and then, for a second time in the history of the world, [we] will have discovered fire."

Got him, Coach.

2.

Hunger

Hunger

A Triptych

1

At night from the rims above Billings, Montana, stars pattern the vault over the Beartooth Range. The Yellowstone River roils unseen in the darkness and the sky is dusted white by the Milky Way turning a slow wheel. Lucky enough to get there early with my father, at sunset a blood red line on the edge of the world parted the horizon under a granite swath of cloud, the sky lit from above, light blue becoming violet, becoming black.

Hunger in the land and sky.

Then nightfall, and him and I seated on rimrock looking south toward the star fields over the Beartooths. In my mind's eye I'm a boy again, and in the dark he's calling me toward something I can't see.

"I'm going to Sylvan Lake tomorrow morning," he says. "You want to go with me?"

I didn't want to go.

I knew it was a five-mile hike up switchbacks as steep as teeth.

But my father persuaded me. We were a fishing family, as comfortable with fly rods as we were with handshakes. Fishing put food on the table. This was one of the first times I remember noticing I was hungry for something other than food. I couldn't put a name to it, but that hunger was a thorn more piercing than physical hunger. Growing up the feeling grew and I felt it equally in the trailer houses we lived in, on the hardwood my brother and I flew over on our way to collegiate and professional basketball, in the rivers we body-floated under white August suns, and atop the mountain passes our father led us through. I felt it on the Northern Cheyenne reservation in southeast Montana where I spent part of my childhood, and at the mouth of Paradise Valley just outside Livingston where I went to high school.

I felt it fishing. I felt it hunting.

That hunger began to permeate my life.

When my father mentioned Sylvan, as a boy I wanted to avoid pain.

He woke me at 4 a.m.

Night dark dreams. His quiet voice. "You ready. Time to get up now."

Bright light over the kitchen table. We poured cereal into thin white bowls. He'd flirted with alcohol, tempted divorce. Drank more. Fought in bars. Divorced my mother for a Crow woman in Plenty Coups south of Billings. Fled the family. Felt broken by the loss of his sons. Left the Crow woman. Remarried my mother.

He leaned over his cereal. Ate his toast. Opened his Bible as if splitting wood.

He read from Proverbs.

For many years, young and old, I'd hated him.

The hunger remained, unspoken, in him and in me.

Hunger can make us more alive. Legend has it the poet and novelist Jim Harrison loved to fish almost as much as he loved women but not quite as much as he loved eating. But I'd say it wasn't hedonism that made him one of America's most recognized voices. It was hunger. Harrison, poorer than he wanted to admit, largely unknown and with limited prospects, had a friend from college days named Tom McGuane. McGuane found early fame with novels like *The Sporting Club*, *The Bushwacked Piano*, and *Ninety-Two in the Shade*, as well as the screenwriting credits for *Rancho Deluxe* and *The Missouri Breaks*. With McGuane's widening Hollywood connections he introduced Harrison to Jack Nicholson. Nicholson asked Harrison to send him something. But Harrison, being unruly, and untrusting of Hollywood, didn't.

A few years later their paths crossed again.

"Why didn't you send me something?" Nicholson asked.

"Because," said Harrison. "People talk but nothing happens. People like yanking people's chains."

Nicholson dug deeper. "How much debt are you in?"

"$16,000," Harrison replied.

"And how much would it take for you to be able to write for a year and not worry about money?"

"$16,000," Harrison said again.

On the spot, Nicholson wrote him a check for $32,000. Harrison went home and wrote *Legends of the Fall* in nine days. The entire novella appeared in *Esquire Magazine*, later becoming one of the nation's most iconic films, starring Anthony Hopkins, Aiden Quinn, Tantoo Cardinal, Julia Ormond, and a young Brad Pitt.

Hunger makes us crazy.

Hunger makes us sane.

At Sylvan, from the trailhead to the first incline is easy. From there it's a sheer grind to the top. We toted our fly rods in dented aluminum tubes, inside us a feeling of light restlessness, hope, and hunger. I was 14, he was 40. When we stopped, we leaned into the rock and drank water, admiring the beauty below, then kept on. Water quiets hunger, but never quite overcomes the hollowness. Hunger is existence, physicality, affection, and the distance between fathers and sons. Climbing mountains to find fish, hunger can also be spiritual hunger. As love grows within you, so beauty grows, the ancients said. For love is the beauty of the soul. We rose through mature lodgepole pines flared at times by stands of aspen, until we left trees behind and moved through switchbacks carved from the mountain wall. Sylvan Lake is a gem more than 9,000 feet high, holding, uncommonly, California golden trout. Stocked in 1938, the fish in Sylvan remain so genetically pure, Montana's Fish and Game still gathers the eggs to stock other lakes. The granite faces of Sylvan Peak ascend another 3000 feet above the water. The first four miles climbing, the gain is so precipitous I start to loath wilderness, despite my best intentions. My father is pleasant all the way, not to spite me, but because he's always taken delight in moving steadily into the sky, a thing common to him nearly his whole life in Montana.

A few hours in, we rest again. Far below we see East Rosebud Lake, the Phantom Creek drainage, and far off the hard span of Froze to Death Plateau, a barrenness covered in snow and ice 11 months of the year where winter winds blow spindrift at hurricane speeds. Today is a blue-sky day, the sun high and hot. Artic gentian blooms mingle with lichen and tough grasses. Crow Lake remains unseen from here, as does the West Rosebud valley and Mystic Lake with its long difficult-to-navigate rock field. The valleys are full of hidden treasures: Huckleberry Lake, Silver Lake, Snow Lakes, Princess Lake and Avalanche Lake, the West Boulder drainage and Island Lake, none of which demand quite the incline Sylvan demands. We walk in country that boasts Tempest Mountain, Mystic Mountain, and Granite Peak—these and hundreds more shoulder the Beartooth Range. In the end, to cut time my father moves us off trail to traverse the edge-wash of a shale ascent where we grab at rock and root and scramble on all fours for a few hundred yards until we top the lip of the bowl. There, we stand, staring down at the bright blue of Sylvan set in the crater. We find sparse trees and hearty scrub brush in the granite swales of the mountain. Sylvan is positioned at the apex of the Hellroaring Creek drainage. The hunger is alive in us now, in our bodies and in all we see. The descent from lip to lake is steep but within the hour we stand near one another setting our lines on the air, schools of goldens visible below the lake's surface in a great clarity of water and light.

2

An elk skull whitened by sun. Flesh and hide eaten away by maggots.

A rack high and wide, spiked, wing-like from the skull plate.

A horn-base thicker than a man's wrist.

Ivory teeth on a Formica tabletop.

If you carry the skull and horns of a bull elk, lifting it by the base of one horn, the bark and heft feel good in the hand, like driftwood but with a heavier core. After a life of mountains and rivers, my hands, like my father's, are meant to carry wild things.

A fish feels like quicksilver, cold, elusive.

Montana: land of mountain ranges, the Beartooths, Crazies, and Bridgers, the Spanish Peaks and the Missions, the Sapphires and Bears Paws. Hunting, like hunger, is visceral. We cleaned animals in the field, always for hunger, also for pride. We used a long narrow hunting knife and a sharpening tool made of metal shaped like a pencil. We split the animal from pelvic crown to neckline and pealed the hide from the body hot. We removed all the edibles, using the rectangular bone saw to remove the quarters. We sawed the head from the spine. If the animal was big we kept the skull and cape for taxidermy. Our hands were steeped in blood.

To curb hunger, we hunted as much as we fished.

Fishing, like hunting, was sustenance, just more fluid and refined. Hunting was violent. Fishing was lightning slicked with water. Dangerous at times but rarely so. The Yellowstone tried to kill me twice, but no doubt the death would have been declared human error. On another occasion, our bird dog, a high-strung Brittany, was swept into rapids. Flailing, she disappeared a mile downstream but eventually came back, her tail between her legs. Fishing meant walking the river in jeans and tennis shoes, moving out shirtless into the pooling water below rock. Leaning back into the flow my father and I made casts that felt like perfection in a world of imperfect things.

We cooked elk and rainbow in a cast iron skillet.

We ate quietly in the evening light of the trailer.

People often ask me what it was like living on the Northern Cheyenne reservation. Scary in the beginning but very good in the end, I say. Lafe Haugen, still close. Russell Tall Whiteman. Cleveland Bement. Blake Walks Nice, murdered behind Jimtown Bar. My brothers. They gave me life.

Trace my family a generation or two and find alcohol in excess, bar fighting, jail time, poverty. Also find love and wilderness. A concentrated amount of that love came from being loved by Northern Cheyenne people. Unknown to me as a boy, the history of the Cheyenne is fraught with genocide. Flying a white flag of peace along with the American flag under Chief Black Kettle, the Cheyenne were massacred at Sand Creek in 1864 by Colonel John Chivington. Chivington and his militia killed women, children, and elders in one of the ugliest engagements in U.S. History, mutilating the bodies, cutting of private parts and later parading them on stage at the Apollo Theatre in Denver along with fetuses and 100 pubic scalps. Chivington, a Methodist deacon, was never brought to justice.

The hunger that lies in the shadow of loss is irrevocable. My family was given more grace than we deserved on the Cheyenne reservation, a line of grace that remains unbroken.

Before I was born, when my father ran with Cleveland Highwalker, also Cheyenne, after my dad had made that trade of deer and magpie for moccasins, after Cleveland's grandmother had dried the skins and chewed the leather to soften it, then sewed precise stitches and set her immaculate beading into the surface, my dad knew love. It is said love is the affinity which draws together the whole world.

My dad's eyes are still haunted. He keeps those moccasins like a talisman, a touchstone.

Hunger is mortality, brotherhood, despair.

Hunger is hope.

3

What do we do with our most insatiable hungers?

When my brother and I were young our father was a teacher and the salary was limited. My father taught fly-fishing at Montana State University and I loved the rhythms, the class in a long line spread out on a low grass field above the campus. Casting vertically toward sunset, soft light setting the lines afire. Accordion-like motion through the chest, cast hand from 10 to 2, draw hand like a bellows moving line below, the cast lengthened to a parabola that released and fell soft as a wish flower on open grass. The days were robin's egg blue, the high plateau of the college held in a red-gold crown of mountains on a full radius around us.

We fished the Yellowstone, the Gallatin, the Jefferson, the Madison.

We cleaned fish on the bank. We were servants of the body, servants of water and light.

Perhaps above all rivers we loved the East Gallatin. To get there we walked through a farmer's field, avoided a Black Angus bull, leapt a low barbed-wire fence and made our way to a set of riffles cascading among cottonwoods, opening on water where fish sparked to the fly. We flew parachute adams, or royal wulff, or wooly buggers. The fly rod vertical and bowlike, the line attached at a bent angle to the water, the fish bolting below the surface. The fight a gift of heaven, my father's big bold laughter ringing off the canyon walls. Hunger is wilderness, and in my father's eyes, wilderness is also peace. Homeward, fish in the creel, the fly rods rattled in the truck bed. Back in the trailer we made simple meals: hunger satisfied by deer and elk filets, rainbow, browns, or cutthroat shaken in a bag of flour with salt and pepper, fried in sticks of butter that made the meat glisten as the coat came up. We ate well, smiling over the day's catch, and afterward we spoke of the river.

Hunger is manifold.

My mom's mother Catherine was Czech and cherished for her powerful effervescent personality and how boldly she loved. Her family having immigrated from the Czech Republic, she was a postmaster for more than four decades on Montana's high plains. She had three main hungers: the love of family, the love of community, and the love of dance. She got two knee replacements in her 70s to keep dancing. On the plains of Eastern Montana she was a force to be reckoned with. She lived 60 miles outside Miles City in a town called Cohagen, an outpost of only two families. Little Dry Creek ran in the draw below her house. Water snakes, dark green with vertical yellow stripes, skated the water's surface. Ant hills stood shin-high, and rattlesnakes rustled through dry grass. Summers with her and my grandfather, we worked cattle, stacked hay, and cleaned rodeo grounds. I remember the dark wood mail slots in her office, her easy way with horsemen, cattlemen, and their families, her cinnamon rolls, and most of all her smile. A rhyme from her homeland stays with me. In Czech, the words are melodic: Beruško, kam poletíš, do peklíčka nebo do nebíčka. In English, the words are more than a little grim:

Ladybird, ladybird, fly away home,

Your house is on fire,

Your children shall burn!

Centuries ago the rhyme was sung by farmers when burning their fields after harvest, urging the ladybird, or ladybug, to fly home, where only one of her children remains, hidden, unburned, under a stone. The ladybug, a sacred symbol of safety from pestilence, beckoned a form of blessing—the hope that one's life work, and thus one's family and children, would be protected. My grandmother soothed me with music and met me with the truth that the world is not always safe. I still hear her voice calling me "miláčku," the Czech word for "darling."

Her mettle was tested not only by tough Montana winters but by the pain harbored in her heritage. In World War II, when Germany invaded the Czech lands, horrors followed. Prague and the Bohemian sections of Czechoslovakia were ruled by Reinhardt Heydrich, personally installed by Hitler. Heydrich's hunger for killing was unquenchable. The Czechs called him the Butcher of Prague, the Blonde Beast. Years into the war, the Czech resistance succeeded in a coup that took Heydrich's life. Hitler's hunger for vengeance followed, and Nazi violence ascended; the massacre at Lidice outside Prague is still considered among the most gruesome in European history. Ten by ten, all men and boys older than 16 were executed by firing squad behind the mayor's barn. One shot to the head, two to the chest. Women were concentrated or killed. Those pregnant were forcibly aborted. In the end, using Magirus gas vans, mechanized death houses referred to in Russian as "душегубка" or "dushegubka," the feminine form for "soul killer," the Nazi's gassed 82 children to death.

Some barely a year old, all younger than 16.

In the aftermath of such sorrow, nothing can console us.

But in shadow and light, other hungers also name us to this world, evoking not hate but a different kind of destiny. As a young woman, my grandmother Catherine fell in love. She married my German grandfather Herbert in New York City during World War II, just after Germany invaded Czechoslovakia. They moved to Montana and square danced through a marriage of more than 50 years. Not without faults, but enduring, and often very loving. Their legacy is a good legacy, their marriage filled of ranching on the high plains of Montana, a general respect and dignity shared with the people around them.

My mother met my father. They loved and fought and lost each other and returned to each other. In between we all lost each other. Harmed and hated each other. Then they humbled themselves and made a new way for the family. Belief was something they took hold of like it held them back from death. They made mountains and water their places of devotion. They influenced me toward a more honest way of life. As if I was a boy learning to dance, they helped me move from mechanical to something more fluid.

As a young man, fly-fishing was a crucial part of this expression—the hunger for the perfect cast a desire even more instinctive than the catch. Increasingly evident in the fast pace of everyday living is the fact that beauty is too often missing from our lives, and this reminds me of water. I see the wilderness not as something to fight against or defeat, not as a masculine adversary, but as feminine, worthy of respect, infinite affection, and our deepest listening. As my father has grown older, he has grown more and more attuned to wilderness, and more and more tender with his sons, and this tenderness has made me more willing to grow. I am often defensive, controlling, stubborn, and too willing to overcome others. Too willing to distance myself when confronted by my own weaknesses, my own failures.

People, and water, have shown me I need to change.

In fly-fishing, the hunger is to cast well, to read rivers, to echo the gracefulness of water. As that hunger grows, it is sometimes accompanied by the will to read the world more gently. National Book Award winning poet Robin Coste Lewis, author of *Voyage of the Sable Venus*, could have been speaking equally of people and the smooth feel of fly-fishing when she said, "Not you and me or us and them, but the world as intimate. There is no other. We are lost together. We are loss. I can tell you anything if it means we can maintain intimacy. Desire is what makes us alive. Your demons knock on your bones. Learn how to be still with yourself. Embodiment means everything. I am a body. I touch other bodies. Pain and limitation. Age and mortality. A lush land of pleasure. Be still."

Here I can believe love is the heart of the wilderness, and wilderness the heart of the world. But in the mountains I'm far from home. I'm with my father who I've spent too many years hurling myself against. I think of my wife and three daughters and all the exquisite men and women I know. I see people wrestling to find a way to love more fully, and I wonder if the truth of us can be captured with regard to that struggle. We are laid low. In my waking dream I turn my face to my wife and ask for help. She calls to me from the living room.

Love with your whole heart.

Let your love be fearless.

I get up from where I am and move toward her, listening.

After my mother and father's tumultuous years, the family struggled through doubt to belief. We began to seek and understand in new ways. The difference was palpable; in our case, we would have disintegrated without it. From there I grew up on the Psalms, through my mom, and the Proverbs, through my dad, as well as many other sacred passages. Something inexpressible in those passages. Words with such an astounding sense of home I fell into them and they gave me the freedom to live.

Many waters cannot quench love. Love is stronger than death.

Surely goodness and mercy shall follow me all the days of my life.

To those who seek understanding, understanding is given.

Love is patient, kind, protects, hopes, endures. Never fails.

I can't wholly comprehend the kindness and power in the lived experience of such words, but I can hear them still, and hear the integrity that exists in their music. Van Gogh said, "The lanterns are burning and the starry night is over all." His vision reminds me of the life of the wilderness that is Montana, and the mountains I've walked with my father to arrive at something good between us.

Hunger is wholeness.

I've been surrounded by good women, my wife, my three daughters, my mother, my wife's mother, my grandmother. Women who call their men to be good men. This mantle of peace is also a descent into darkness, a dense and abiding darkness in which the light emerges in words and the cadence of words and a poetry whose melody is the breathing of my wife and daughters in the evening as they fall asleep. I feel deeply loved by how my wife's face is illumined from the light in the hall, and I remember when she spoke to me before I went out to meet my father. It's not for you, she whispered, it's for your daughters. The souls of others. How I pressed my face to hers and felt the bones of her cheek against mine, the bones of her forehead and the orbital bones of her eyes, the kiss of her lips against the underside of my wrist.

She kissed me to grant life, and to ward off death.

That day on Sylvan Lake my father and I touched mountains, water, and sky.

But we caught no fish.

Life humbles us, just as love calls us to this world.

A man who'd come up earlier gave us a few of his goldens before he ascended and topped the ridge and was gone. Kindness in the wilderness. Toward late afternoon, my dad and I sat together eating over a small fire, happy to receive sustenance.

What hungers make us whole? What losses change the arc of our lives?

I'm willing to believe the generosity of Cleveland Highwalker and Lafe Haugen, of my wife, my grandparents, and my father and mother, of Jim Harrison's gift and of the wilderness around us, is one generosity—calling forth hunger, answering hunger with life, pressing into my hand like the tensile body of a cutthroat I put on the stringer and clean at the water's edge at day's end.

Through every cleft the world we perceive floods us with its riches, Teilhard de Chardin said—

> ...food for the body, nourishment for the eyes, harmony of sounds and fullness of the heart, unknown phenomena and new truths, all these treasures, all these stimuli, all these calls, coming to us from the four corners of the world, cross our consciousness at every moment. What is their role within us? What will their effect be, even if we welcome them passively or indistinctly, like bad workmen? They will merge into the most intimate life of our soul and either develop it or poison it. We only

have to look at ourselves for one moment to realize this, and either feel delight or anxiety.

Hunger makes us seek, keeps us vital, strikes the soul, makes fire.

I believe our primary hunger is love. Even now when I look to the night sky, I recall my father's gentleness. Something I'd left unremembered for years.

The star fields over these mountains lead me home.

My Dad, in America

Your hand on my jaw
but gently

and that picture
of you punching through snow
to bring two deer, a gopher,

and a magpie
to the old Highwalker woman

who spoke only Cheyenne
and traced our footprints

on leather she later chewed to soften.
We need to know in America there is still blood

for forgiveness.
Dead things for the new day.

3.

On Suffering

After We Lose Our Mothers, What's Left?"

Sheldon McLain[1] at his strongest and most authentic was not only a man of uncommon interior discipline, but a physical specimen worthy of the celebrated, even archetypal images of the masculine. Half Cree, half Irish, he stood 6 feet 4 inches tall, intimidating when angry, but often lovely in everyday life. Coarse black hair. Eyes dark over a muscular frame. He died young, in his thirties, in a car accident on the winter roads of the Highline in northern Montana. For many years he had been my close friend, a complex person, mercurial, at times confusing, at times winsome, hard to understand and stubborn enough to be difficult. Capable of grave harms, he lived a double life wrought by generational cycles of abuse and pain. A seeker, in Sheldon's most hard-fought moments he evoked compassion and openness.

With respect for his death, I want to speak of his life.

---

[1] Sheldon McLain was a participant in my doctoral research at the University of Alberta in Canada, a hermeneutic phenomenological investigation on the essence of the forgiving touch. Sheldon gave his written consent for his participation and asked that he not be given a pseudonym but that I use his real name in the dissertation and whenever his story appeared in print.

Viktor Frankl conceived of three elements every person must face and resolve to find meaning. Frankl's tragic triad is comprised of pain, guilt, and suffering. How we face these generational and humanity-wide inner storms builds our capacity to heal or be healed and sustains our desire to love and be loved. In coming to a better understanding of life we must pass through the history of our mothers and fathers. Our choices in this regard are of paramount importance.

Sheldon McLain, in the following story, revealed the integrity of such choices.

Shel and I first met as boys on the Northern Cheyenne reservation in southeast Montana.

My father was the head basketball coach and high school principal at St. Labre, the students a combination of Northern Cheyenne from Lame Deer, Busby, and Ashland, and those from the Crow Nation bused in from Crow Agency, Pryor, and Lodge Grass.

I found out from Sheldon his father died due to drug-related events just before I arrived on the Cheyenne reservation. As young boys, Sheldon and his older brother George were left in the care of the State. Sheldon's mother, a full-blown alcoholic living in Canada, did not come to retrieve them. Eventually the two boys were adopted by a white family in Ashland, the small mill town that bordered the reservation. Ironically, Sheldon attended a white grade school while I attended a Cheyenne grade school.

We saw each other often, we loved basketball, and we played the game all out. Our heroes were the players who starred for my father's team: young men with names that matched the originality they showed on the court—Juneau

Plenty Hawk, Fred and Paul Deputy, Willie Gardner, Stanford Rides Horse. We grew up admiring them and trying to emulate them, and then my family moved away, and Sheldon and I lost touch.

Years later, both of us having left the reservation, having lived in totally different geographic regions spanning America, Europe, and Canada, we met again and discovered common ground and formed a lasting friendship. We both pursued collegiate basketball and ended up spending a decade of summers coaching younger players on the summer basketball camp circuit. We also both pursued graduate degrees in psychology and spent countless hours talking about the inner life, family, and God. Sheldon's boyhood trauma revealed a harsh truth I'd found from reading Rowe, Halling, and other researchers: "the need for forgiveness arises when someone has acted in such a way as to bring about a fundamental disruption to the wholeness or integrity of one's life. Initially, on a deep, almost organic level, there is a tearing of the fabric of one's life, one's world." The mother loss and father loss Sheldon experienced, both of acute severity, formed a complex network of internal pain and the desire to overcome. Near the end of completing my PhD in psychology when I began researching touch and forgiveness, I asked Sheldon if I could interview him.

His story is printed below in his own words.

I'd been dealing with those emotions of resentment and abandonment the years between my father taking me away from my mom when I was about three and then the possibility of seeing her for the first time again at 18. There was a lot of years there, a lot of gradual healing took place, and as I got older, I think I was able to work through some of those feelings slowly and by the time I was 18, yes I was very nervous, but I had pretty much come to terms with a lot of the abandonment. I had been given a home. Through the State I had been blessed with two parents who cared for me, provided for me, gave me opportunities to succeed in life, and I had been around other people that also furthered that and really focused their love to meet my needs and to help me in my areas of weakness. Areas such as the insecurity that comes from abandonment. I'd started to believe in myself and not be ashamed but accept and actually be proud of my past. As a Native American Indian I had a heritage to be proud of.

But I was afraid.

She called me and said she was coming to my brother's wedding. So she came down four weeks later. And during those four weeks—in between the time she called and the wedding—I prayed every night. My prayer was along the lines of, "God, I really need your help in this, I need your love because I don't have any love for her in my own heart. I want to be able to say I love you Mom, to her. And I want that to be genuine and I want it to be strong—not something that is just said. So I ask you to give me your love so that I may be able to show her your love and that you would just work in me and do whatever it takes."

I prayed this prayer every night before falling asleep, for a month. At the end of the time she came down to the wedding, and I was taken aback by her appearance. I remembered her as a little child would, when I was three years old. That was the last time I'd seen her. I remembered her as being young and pretty, and she had long black hair and she was tall and she had a beautiful face, and being Native Canadian Indian, being Cree, she had dark skin and dark eyes, and she was a pretty lady. But the first time I saw her at the wedding it was amazing. I was taken aback by the changes. Her face showed a lot of pain, a lot of years. Her face was just haggard—it was hard and there was no light in her eyes. Nothing that showed joy. There was nothing that showed happiness. And that was a day that she should have been rejoicing; her son was getting married. She was hardened. Like she just didn't show emotion, it was just harsh. She'd had a hard life as evidenced by her face; she's got a lot of scars you know. And a lot of those scars are because of what she did, because of the pain of living without your son. She's a fairly tall lady, about 5'11" and she still had long black hair. You could tell that she'd been pretty once, but there was nothing now that would really be attractive. She kind of stooped when she walked and there was no confidence in her. That weekend we probably spent about six to seven total hours together, during which I smelled alcohol on her breath constantly. I remember the night after the wedding we went back to the hotel. She had to pick up some clothes, and when I walked into her hotel room it smelled like a liquor store. It was the stench of alcohol, of hard liquor, the same that was on her breath. I remember walking out of her hotel room and just saying to myself, it's no big deal you know, no big deal.

The next day she was leaving and it was about 10:30 in the morning. I remember standing in my foster-parents' living room. Everyone had gathered there to say their goodbyes, and she was nervous, you could tell. She was kind of hesitant, shifting back and forth and I was also pretty nervous. I was praying the whole time to myself, just, God, I'm going to be strong, I'm going to be strong. I was pretty emotional; I was ready to cry. My mom stood across the room and... here's her 18-year-old son. She's never been a part of his life, she's had no contact whatsoever, and she's never heard the words I love you come out of his lips. And I'm sure she's scared of rejection. I'm sure she's scared of a lot of things. We'd never talked openly about her alcohol or anything like that, it was just kind of a skirted issue. Then she said, "Well, we've got to be going now, we've got a long road ahead of us. We have to drive back to Canada and it's about a nine-hour drive." She was making small talk and she was kind of at a standstill, she didn't know what to say. I walked across the room, took about three steps, and put my arms out and she took a step toward me. I embraced her and said, "I love you, Mom."

It was the only time I had embraced her and it was a real strong moment. My left arm was underneath her right arm and my right arm would be on top of her shoulder. Her hair was kind of in my face, it was real close. Our bodies were close to one another and I remember having my hand on her back and just drawing her to me and holding her strongly for a while. I made sure it felt strong, not weak. It was like the ending part of the story of forgiveness—for my forgiveness of her you know.

It was just healing for me to reach out and say, I love you, Mom.

It was like saying I forgive you, I love you... it's okay.

The embrace had a lot to do with forgiveness of all those years of abandonment and pain, and hatred towards her. The touch was an acknowledgement of the relationship that existed between us as a son and a mother. That bond had been re-established and recognized and acknowledged in the eyes of others. If I was giving her something, I was giving her her son back… in the sense that I was giving my heart to her as a son and looking at her as my mother. I was acknowledging that she was my mother yet realizing at the same time she most likely wouldn't act on that and she wouldn't involve herself any differently after we touched. I gave her the freedom and the opportunity to be there. And for that moment in time she was my mother.

City on the Threshold of Stars

A Triptych

1

1942. Over the wide grey ocean back to Prague and the River Vltava in central Bohemia, the Mother of Cities, the Golden City, City on the Threshold of Stars. To Nazi occupation, where I wonder where I came from and watch the world grow smaller and bigger at once, the violent enthroned in the seat of nations, a tongue for the song of women and men, to halt the old order and inscribe the new with consuming fire. Jan Kubiš and Jozef Gabčík, soldiers, sons of Czech, born for a day when the body rises and kills and the mouth long silent shouts vengeance to the sky. My three daughters were not yet born. My three daughters were yet to be when an entire city was lost. Removed from the face of the earth. My grandfather Herbert is German. My grandmother Catherine is Czech. The cloth they wore was common.

In secret, the Czech king commissioned Jan and Jozef to travel nocturnal by foot and boat, over mountains and rivers through the dark west to England, to be welcomed by the old-century Royal Air Force and given the new science to return to their besieged country, hunt, find, and destroy the devil Heydrich, the Nazi warlord, the Butcher of Prague.

City on a hill, Lidice, small Prague on the flat south of the high mountains called Pyratetten. Teeth of the Sky. Of Czech blood venerable, laid bare, and borne of love. By faith, the Czechs believed. By fate, it came to be.

Nazi onslaught obscuring day, bearing night to the capital city of nations, Prague, foreign tanks and airbirds, fears and terrors, skies filled of fire and screaming bombs, wind-cleavers, the cry of children and the mother's wail, mobs, sirens, no water, thirst, they covered their heads, suffered, waited for England, for allies, but in the end, their land was taken. The unthinkable, to be lost to Germany.

My young daughter once said you're my favorite Daddy in the stars.

She didn't know how Prague and her people sought Heydrich, the Blond Beast, to take his life and return him whole to hell—the familiar hand of the final solution, the uniform he kept clean, narrow-nosed man whose wife, dog-eyed and supple, reminded the living of another Nazi frau who made lampshades of Jewish skin, Hangman Heydrich who adored power, wanted his boss Himmler's life, and took the thousand-year throne of the Bohemian kings at Hradschin Castle high over the St. Charles Bridge.

2

My daughters didn't know, to emulate the Fuhrer Heydrich slaughtered Czechs. Jan, of average height, thin-faced, serious, Jozef, bigger, boisterous, wide-chested, willing when called to forfeit their lives.

"Tomorrow, we end it," Jan shouted over the propeller noise.

"Tomorrow," Jozef answered, looking to the eyes of his friend.

"Are you afraid?"

Jan took Jozef's face in his hands.

"Today, we die well my friend."

Their clothing was dark, the face of Heydrich emblazoned in the mind's eye as the aircraft droned on.

"Why do I love you so much?" I asked my daughter, three times.

"Because God made you to love me," she said, and still so young she didn't yet know how fully, how completely, beautiful things synchronize.

When the Nazis invaded the Czech lands my Czech grandmother married my German grandfather in New York City where they danced and heard little word of their home countries but let their bodies flare like flame in the dark of the dance hall as they tipped their heads to the light and kissed with abandon.

I am German. I am Czech.

Night drop at low altitude in a British plane, two men on strings fell down and down in darkness, the land below like a lost love, laskah, returned to the earth effortless as shadows. Near invisible, near light the men ran as those who know their enemy and whose desire is to destroy him.

On a morning in May when Heydrich drove his green Mercedes coupe toward the Castle in Prague, the two leapt from a corner, concealed, lofted their British-made bomb and blew the rear of the car to pieces, shattering Heydrich's spine. The Butcher wrinkled his nose. Groans slipped from the slit of his mouth.

Fire, whispered Jan, and Jozef beheld the beauty billowing, mixed with smoke, a red black column tunneling the sky. Can we ever really know each other? My daughters. Me. The men who fled cursing Heydrich in his death throes, leaving him for what they hoped was God's reckoning, the uniform he kept clean, blood-soaked, tattered, the Butcher's body, the Butcher's face. He breathed for ten days and when he died of his wounds Hitler summarily executed one-thousand, three-hundred thirty-one Czechs.

Two-hundred one women among them.

The Nazis besieged Jan and Jozef and others of the Czech resistance in the Karl Borromaeus Church, and no Czechs came out alive. The Germans took three-thousand Jews from the safe ghetto at Theresienstadt and herded them East to be exterminated. Five-hundred of the six-hundred at large Jews in Berlin were imprisoned and on the day of Heydrich's death one-hundred fifty-two were executed.

Can we ever forget the small village, Lidice, near the mining town Kladno, and how the Germans marched to avenge their Heydrich? The town twelve miles from Prague. The raiment, the clothing of the children—no one knows where it went. To our shame now we have nearly forgotten Hitler's orders:

1. Execute all men by shooting.

2. Send all women to concentration camps.

3. Concentrate the children.

4. Those capable of being Germanized send to SS families in Germany.

5. Burn the town and level it to the ground.

Three days after Heydrich's heart stopped, ten flights of German Security Police under the command of Captain Max Rostock took formation around the village. Nine years later, Rostock hung by the neck in Prague, but first from the bullhorn his loud voice in the German tongue.

3

"Alles muss hier bleiben!"

Everyone stays.

"Keine gehen!"

No one goes.

From dawn to dusk Nazi soldiers led boy and man to the garden behind the Mayor's barn to be shot by firing squad at close range. Tap, tap, tap. Three bullets: head, chest, chest. Ten of the living at a time. One-hundred seventy-two men and boys. Their bodies like leaves on the ground. Spiritbone.

The German Police took seven Lidice women to Prague and shot them in public. City of One-hundred Spires. The remainder, one-hundred ninety-five women in all, they sent to Ravensbrück where seven met the gas chamber, three disappeared, and forty-two expired from concentration camp conditions.

Of the Lidice women, an unlucky four were pregnant, my daughters still don't know those women were taken to a hospital in Prague, their children forcibly aborted, the women shipped empty to Ravensbrück.

I hope my daughters never know how the Germans took the living children of Lidice to a concentration camp, ninety in all. I am Czech. Spiritbone. I am German. From these, Himmler's "racial experts" deemed eight children sound, garment of praise, and they were sent to Germany to be raised German with German names. Ingested into the Fatherland through the Nazi program Lebensborn.

The remaining eighty-two children were taken by train to Lodz where they lived three weeks in a collection camp, the youngest, only a year and six days old, the oldest boys fourteen, the oldest girls fifteen. In early June, they arrived at a castle where they were told to undress, keep only underwear, a towel, and a bar of soap for a shower before the journey to Chelmno.

The children were then squeezed into the closed bed of a truck modified to fit ninety bodies and killed by exhaust in eight minutes. My three daughters are Czech. To name God is to be separate from God. My three daughters are German. To name God is to name love. Natalya. Ariana. Isabella. When you were born, I kissed the skin on the inside of your wrists and whispered, I will love you forever. How like your mother you are! So ready to defend mankind. I see you hand in hand looking out over the edge of the world to a land beyond our reach. At war's end no trace of Lidice remained: the houses bonfired, the ruins dynamited, the rubble covered by landfill. All men killed. All women and children abducted, forsaken, or exterminated.

The earth under storm and rain, snow and broken tree, a rose garden, silence. The ground the garment of praise instead of the spirit of despair. As late as 1947, the last women of Lidice sent newspaper pleas through Allied media into post-war German homes: My city was lost. My child taken. Please return my child. I am from Lidice. Our husbands were shot. Our children lost.

Have mercy on us.

And some few boy-children were returned home not knowing their mothers' names.

4.

Fathers

Hellroaring Plateau

A Quintet

1

I think of my father's hands, like a map of their own wilderness.

As a boy I walked with my father along the Yellowstone River on the northern edge of the Beartooth Range in southern Montana. We walked with purpose and looked intently into the clear pools. Sun filled the basin. The land held the gold and silver of grasses, hardy cottonwoods along the river, the black and grey of rock promontories, and the dark green of forests that reached behind us to the sky.

I was 15 and the world was new. A freshman in high school, manhood seemed far off. Into the river we went. Up to the waist in water, I felt contained by water and light. I wore jeans and old shoes. The river flowed around me. Bare-chested, I leaned back and the water held me in place. I was small. The river was big. My father stood upstream in a flash of sun over the ripples. A giant. A shadow. He moved his hands over the water. A parachute adams, brown bodied, with rust in the tail and the signature white crown, flew overhead and came to rest on the water at the top of a draw below a large rock. My father's line jumped and bowed, moonlike from his outstretched arm, and he joyfully called to me. I shouted back to him. He drew a rainbow from the river and we smiled and laughed and kept on until we had enough for dinner.

Balance this against the aggression we too often felt for each other, that and my own fears of life without him leading me. Fly fishing is a subcurrent of life, or perhaps it is all of life, a passage strewn with daunting obstacles, brambles and gnarled trees, cut banks and the laddered spill of whitewater carving its descent through rock. Smoothness in the outflow. My father and I have always loved rivers. In the demanding presence of a landscape too bold to be named, the art of fishing, of becoming a good fly fisher, is not something that occurs quickly. My own early failures fly fishing remind me in their way of distrust and incomprehension, emotionally blunt instruments through which every fish seems to pass beyond reach. And yet we improve. We gain headway. Sometimes our fathers lead us deeper into the realization that a line laid down with precision and elegance over good water contains unforeseen possibility.

There is a wilderness in me and my father, and in the life of everyone I know. In Montana the sun fills the sky with light. The loop of the line and the fall of an adams parachute, the miniscule lie of the white tuft on the surface of the big river, the rise of something from unforeseen depth. On the water a sincere call is followed by an ecstatic response—and one almost hears the world asking us to leave ourselves behind, the ache of our woundedness, the unrelenting fires and great losses. Can we love others more than we thought possible? Can we atone for the distance between us? When I see my father in the long light of evening, the river purling at his waist and the fluid arc of his arm in the sky, affirmation speaks, unexpected and steadfast, and sets the soul at ease.

2

Wilderness is winter.

A man found frozen to death on a fence line.

A woman pierced through the eye by the tine horn of a bull moose.

Jawbone of a lynx.

Beak of a crow.

In the wilderness of the high country I encounter the wilderness of the human heart. Life is made of remoteness and threat, closeness and unimagined beauty.

Wilderness is also spring. The sound of water.

The scent of lupine and shooting star, paintbrush, and wood lily.

3

In an America often brimming with disdain, a thin veil for inner despair, what is hope? And where does hope reside? For me, hope lives in the mountains. Contrary to the hyper-speed of the contemporary age, in the mountains I've found there are those who walk toward the dawn, traversing the night's darkness to emerge unafraid.

In contemporary America, irony is the breeding ground where we first begin to feel comfortable placing others and the world we inhabit under the cold eye of our contempt. Certainly, irony is the more raucous and less easily controlled brother of healthy skepticism, but without health we collude in our own collective inertia and inch forward until we fall like detritus over the lip of a yawning abyss and finally reach what Wallace Stegner famously referred to as our angle of repose. With the current rate of physical, emotional, and familial deficit, mass environmental destruction, and a war and prison economy equaled only by what Mother Theresa once called America's spiritual poverty, where do we look to find a sense of hope if hope is what we need? Mother Theresa's indictment was even more barbed than we might imagine: she said America is the poorest country because America's poverty is spiritual poverty.

Hope.

We find it in the least likely places. At dusk when the sky's burden moves from blue to black. At dawn when, from far below, the vault is filled with light. Or perhaps we find hope down one of those high country roads we knew we needed to walk but were afraid to for fear of what we might find. In Montana, the history of then and the reality of now attends us. There is the fraught path of Euro-American influence, and the more subtle and also fraught path of the sovereign nations who first called Montana home: the Crow, Northern Cheyenne, Dakota, Gros Ventre, Assiniboine, Chippewa-Cree, Blackfeet, Salish, Kootenai, Pend d'Oreille, and Little Shell Chippewa. Nations with their own names largely unuttered by those unfamiliar to them: the Apsáalooke, Tsitsistas, Yankton, Aaniiih, Hohe, Ne Hiyawak, Siksikaitsitapi, Séliš, Ktunaxa, Qlispé, Esens

Ojibwe. Finally, there are the many peoples who inhabit Montana's boundaries from throughout the world who hope to make a life in a place more remote than most.

The Nez Perce too, or Nimi'ipuu, have a Montana legacy of rare and uncommon fortitude lesser known to dominant American culture. In this sense, the imprint of those who came before us is the imprint of those who lead us on.

Ten miles west of Wisdom, Montana, in far southwest Montana there are miracles of topography painfully beautiful to the eye. The Rockies run north to south. In late Autumn, if we have the courage, we might walk together into the night to see what we can see. The night is long and the path uneven and often precarious but on the other side light awaits. In the pre-dawn black massive fortresses of rock are ominous and ever present, while forests shroud the land in silence. When the sun lights the world, the mountains are a strange and otherworldly architecture filled of air and refracted light, towering sculptures of stone carved as if from a profound excess of materials. Above and to the west the red sky burns on the jagged edge of the earth and when the sun finally breaks the eastern horizon our shoulders tilt and our bodies turn gold.

Here we are returned to the world with gratitude.

And ten miles west of Wisdom, Montana, there are miracles of human friendship and good will to marvel the miracles of the sky. Consider Robbie Paul, a modern-day Nez Perce woman who knew the depths of atrocity her people experienced. Consider her story, a woman whose family had suffered unimaginable loss, and who discovered the only road out was to pass through an honest and heart-wrenching encounter with the history of genocide endured by her people. Consider that she also knew she needed to walk that road hand in hand with her father.

In a time fraught with violent upheavals in the nation and across the globe, we can listen to Robbie's story, and let her lead us to a place of right feeling again. There are people who speak a deep and meaningful truth. Robbie Paul, Nez Perce, is a direct descendant of Chief Joseph, the man who spoke his words of irrevocable gravity on the Trail of Tears: "Hear me, my chiefs: my heart is sick and sad. From where the sun now stands, I will fight no more forever." Robbie Paul is Nez Perce, a people of uncommon tenacity in the unfolding of United States history. She is a member of a sovereign nation who now holds reconciliation ceremonies at the site of the Big Hole Massacre, ten miles west of Wisdom, Montana, where little more than a century ago, Nez Perce men, women, and children were massacred by U.S. military.

After the Battle of the Clearwater, Nez Perce leaders had moved their people across a vast expanse of wilderness, trying to escape the soldiers of General Oliver Otis Howard. They went from Idaho into Montana through the brutal terrain of Lolo Pass. After another small skirmish with U.S. military they entered the Bitterroot Valley and proceeded south. Looking Glass had been installed in leadership, succeeding Chief Joseph for a brief span along the journey. Looking Glass gave his oath to the white settlers in the Bitterroot Valley that his people would pass through with no violence. He kept his promise. There, the settlers traded with him and he was able to purchase supplies from some of the merchants.

Looking Glass convinced his people that Howard was far behind and that the citizens of Montana did not want war, so the Nez Perce took their time, did not prepare a rear guard, and failed to send out scouts or set reconnaissance protecting their encampments. On the other side of the Bitterroot Valley, the Nez Perce topped a mountain range and descended into the Big Hole Basin where they used the forest there to replenish their tipi poles.

In an unforeseen and withering turn, a different military detachment under Colonel John Gibbon was already on the way from Fort Shaw with 161 men and one Howitzer. At night he and his men marched through the mountains, hoping to find the encampment before dawn. Following the trail of the Nez Perce, Gibbon gained 45 civilian volunteers from the Bitterroot Valley and proceeded until he discovered the Nez Perce encampment in the Big Hole.

His orders: no prisoners, no negotiations.

Gibbon took position overlooking the Nez Perce. It was still night, with 89 tipis arranged in a V-shaped pattern on the far side of the North Fork of the Big Hole River. The sound and sheen of water between Gibbon and the tribe. Through willow and wild sage, the soldiers approached before daylight. They encountered an elderly Nez Perce man and killed him, then moved quietly through waist-high water to cross the river. When they emerged on the far shore, they rushed the village and laid gunfire into the tipis where the Nez Perce were sleeping. Taken by surprise the Nez Perce fled as Gibbon's troops fired indiscriminately, killing nearly 90 people, most of them women and children.

Those who escaped were led north by Chief Joseph.

Chief Joseph's final pronouncement came in the Bears Paw Mountains not far from Canadian border. By his actions throughout his life and specifically on the Trail of Tears, a leader recognized as one of the finest leaders in American history confirmed the tenacity and valor of the Nez Perce.

Unimaginable if it weren't for the fact that it's true, today the Nez Perce have shaped the site of the Big Hole massacre into a place of hope recognized throughout the world as among the most graceful and solemn places of human dignity. With the resolve to help heal the heart of the world, today the descendants of those who were massacred invite the descendants of the U.S. military who committed the massacre to walk together with them, carrying lanterns through the dark into the dawn. Each year, at sunrise, a ceremony of peace is performed. The Nez Perce invite reconciliation. People confront their fears and emerge stronger and more capable. Despite every right to be hateful or violent, the Nez Perce forgive, drawing the human race into a necessary encounter with our own darkness. They take the veil from our eyes and let us see.

They touch our brokenness and make us whole again.

Today, Robbie Paul, a scholar with a PhD in leadership studies from Gonzaga University, lives in the Spokane area just north of Deer Park and is a professor at Washington State University. In her doctoral research she traced five generations of Nez Perce leaders in her own family, from the advent of first white contact to today. From Chief Joseph's resolute leadership of her people, to the quiet power of her own leadership, she found the resilience and intrepid communal wisdom of her people. She found in her people the road to healing, even in the face of genocide and dislocation. A long road, and one that requires our most vital will. Her head lifted, she saw water, land, and sky. Her hands knew the design of aspen and poplar, bull pine, cottonwood, lodgepole. At the end of her journey she took her father's hand and walked into the heart of the mountains where she sat down with him and with the descendants of those who had massacred her people and her father's people.

There she did not offer cynicism or contempt, revenge or ruin.

She and her father offered peace.

And when they looked to the rim of the world, their faces shone like fire.

4

If the crux of our experience with life and one another could be captured in a phrase, it might be found in the words of Herman Hesse:

Children live on one side of despair, the awakened on the other.

I am reminded of the beloved women and men in my life who have shown me that true living is inevitably tied to a painful awakening. My father contains great wildernesses. In the mountains of Montana, the sun is big and close, and shines bright in a seemingly endless sky. There, the sun rises like a champion, delighting to run his course. Likewise, when the heart is illumined we become more present to ourselves and the world around us. In this sense, receiving light evokes the experience of what Hesse referred to as being *awakened.*

Consider the wilderness of self-discovery. Alone in small-town Montana as a boy I felt overwhelming fear, like something threadbare over the imminent threat of violence. I needed the larger world to raise me up into new understandings. The wilderness of marriage, its visions, threats, and communion further opened me and returned me to the consolations and desolations of my own family history. Those who encountered wasteland and became bitter people. Those who sought peace. My cousin's descent to an addictive underworld and the finality of her death in a drug shootout on the streets of Billings. Uncles and aunts, old and alone after being burned as if by fire, alongside those whose single or married lives drew them to a larger humanity. My Czech grandmother Catherine's marriage to my German grandfather Herbert, two who danced at the beginning, and danced throughout their more than 50 year marriage, as if refined by the tragic events of their own cultural histories.

The human wilderness, like the mountains we know, is made up of shadow and light. Because of my grandmother and her old European sensibilities, the wider world beyond the American West always called to me. After college, I moved to Germany, and here the human wilderness came more alive. Often my thoughts had seemed caught in a rut of place, unable to escape the confines of the American West. By learning more of my family's genocidal bloodline, Germany dislocated me and helped right me again.

America's dominant culture can be self-embedded, and yet the world cries out against my own self-embeddedness.

Consider another story, set also in World War II, and attuned to Hesse's concept of awakening. Viktor Frankl was a contemporary of Hesse. Born in 1902 in Vienna, Frankl became one of the leading neurologists in Europe, serving as head neurologist in the Selbstmörderpavillon or "suicide pavilion" of the General Hospital in Vienna. He treated more than 30,000 women prone to suicide, and when the Nazis invaded Austria and he was relegated to practicing medicine only with Jews, he continued his neurology work, also worked as a brain surgeon, and succeeded in giving medical opinions that saved many patients from being euthanized during the span in which Nazis routinely found and killed the handicapped and the mentally ill.

When the Nazi regime grew stronger in Vienna, Viktor's parents arranged for his exile in America. Viktor, however, was not sure he should go. If he went to America his parents would face a very difficult future, but his life would be saved. If he stayed in Austria he could act as a buffer to serve and protect them. He agonized over the decision and in the end decided to wait for a Divine answer. When only days remained before he must decide, Viktor came home and found his father seated at the kitchen table with a piece of rubble in front of him. Viktor asked what happened and his father told him the Nazis had destroyed the temple that day. From where Viktor stood he saw a symbol engraved on the piece of broken rock, a mark his father had not yet noticed. Looking closely, Viktor made it out: the mark was a number from the Ten Commandments, the number for the commandment *honor your father and mother.*

As I discovered this, I was convinced it meant Viktor would go to America for exile.

Viktor remained with his parents until he and they were taken from each other and shipped to separate concentration camps. His obedience was deeper, more in harmony with the soul. In the concentration camps at Theresienstadt, Auschwitz, and Türkheim, on labor detail after being separated from his parents and his wife, Frankl worked until the final moments of the war to prevent suicide in his fellow prisoners and to try to cure them of depression and weariness of life. Inside the terrible night of the Holocaust, Frankl lost his wife and family. He walked in wilderness. When he emerged on the other side, from his stark bereavement he called on the words of World War I poet Anton Wildgans who said:

What is to give light must endure burning.

When we face the fearful adversity of our collective existence, human wilderness desolates or consoles, but inevitably awakens us. The novelist Hesse and the survivor Frankl, along with the Nez Perce American leader Robbie Paul—the first invoking the imagined landscape, the second two a tangible and unfathomable reality—impart a well-discerned sense of this complex and highly charged world. As if from sleep we are awakened, and like the mountains we hold dear, like the mountains that hold us, Herman Hesse and Robbie Paul speak to us, and Viktor Frankl reminds us of the magnificent, if tragic, ethos of who and what we are:

> Man is that being who invented the gas chambers of Auschwitz; however, he is also that being who entered those chambers upright, with the Lord's Prayer or the Shema Yisrael on his lips.

5

As I grew to adulthood, I distanced myself from my father.

Looking back, I see myself lost in the wilderness between us.

My life changed when I fell in love with my wife, Jennifer. Her feminine essence mingled with the masculine in me and taught me how to live, and my love for my father experienced a resurgence.

When I conducted research on the essence of touch and forgiveness I wanted to understand the concrete experience of the moment when we touch another in the attempt to forgive, or when we are touched by another and feel forgiven. From a philosophical perspective, the work involved interpreting the lived experience of when touch and forgiveness coincide. People harm each other. Some never recover. But for those who encounter forgiveness, a new understanding of freedom emerges. In wilderness, my skin is torn by jagged surfaces. There is darkness and dawn. And in human wilderness there is the same ruggedness, perhaps only slightly less tangible—toward smoothness and fracture, rest, roughness, fusion, reunion. Touch and forgiveness inform each other in elegant and sonorous ways, and with my wife I found their unity among the great gifts to humanity.

When a son, for example, seeks forgiveness and atonement from his own father, the quest is impossible if that son has not humbled himself. Likewise, a father's atonement is confirmed by his humility, his gentleness. The real family work fathers and sons go through results in what Ignatius called peace of soul, a well lived life of meaningful touch, an embodied sense of emotional, verbal and physical healing; justice and mercy in the aftermath of harm; and a holistic fusion of the feminine and the masculine. Grace leads us to where the fear of wilderness subsides and is subsumed by intimacy.

When someone becomes transparent, sincerely asks forgiveness or offers forgiveness, and chooses the long journey to atonement, we witness the miracle of human existence. When I think of this miracle I often think of my daughters' hands. Then I think of the hands of others. Hands in all shades and sizes, all ages and states of loveliness or disrepair. The hand is a symbol of our shared humanity toward one another: the hand of violence, the hand of peace, the hand on which a finger is broken or cut-off, the hand that is young and new to the world, the old and weather-worn hand. The hand that has been amputated. Hands are vessels of despair or vessels of hope. Even when we are bound by fear our humanity calls out to one another.

Jennifer asked me once, not have you forgiven your father, but have you *asked forgiveness* of him?

"Of course not," I replied. "If anyone needs to ask forgiveness it's him."

"You're wrong," she said plainly.

Exasperated, I said "What would I need to ask forgiveness for?"

"Contempt," she said. "For the contempt you hold in your heart against him. For how rarely you speak love to him. How rarely you touch him."

Our hands display our humanity or lack thereof.

The level of violence the world presently faces is tantamount to a collective epidemic of annihilation. Three centuries ago, there were 5 million war related deaths, and two centuries ago, 20 million. But with the industrial age, in an astonishingly violent laying on of hands humanity has experienced 110 million war related deaths in the past century. Add in government-imposed genocides and government-imposed famines and the number reaches a staggering 180 million.

We know ultimate evil exists. What is less reported or given less narrative voice is ultimate intimacy, and ultimate reconciliation. In current social science research forgiveness is now being revealed as the systemic and biological counter to the violence that exists in the world. As alluded to earlier, researchers such as Enright, Worthington, McCullough, and DiBlasio have linked higher forgiveness capacity to less anxiety, less depression, less heart disease, and greater emotional well-being, with new research moving toward linking greater forgiveness capacity to stronger immune systems.

The path from war to peace is arduous and hard won.

Again I see my father's hands, their strange topography, their wilderness.

I think of my hands echoing his, and my daughters' hands echoing mine.

The wilderness of the American Northwest and Inland Northwest is a corridor of land and sky that runs from Oregon to Washington, from Alaska to British Columbia, from Alberta to Idaho to my home state of Montana. The Northwest is also a crucible. Spending time with my dad in the high country, letting the landscape absorb me has given me an abiding reverence for the intricacy and grandeur of the natural world. Awe and violence, emptiness, death and life, intimacy: all are aspects of our relationship to landscape and to each other. In spring, the land casts off a heavy cloak of snow revealing the shed horns and scattered ribwork of elk and deer. The orbital casing in the skull of an eagle. Before long, wildflowers bloom and blanket the mountains. Both landscape and people are breathtaking, calling us back as if from a long slumber, casting off dread. In the seasonal advance from wildflowers to dry grass, from the autumn trees carrying dusk in their arms to the winds of winter, eloquent questions attend life in Montana both in the mountains and in the heart. From poet Mary Oliver:

Tell me, what is it you plan to do
with your one wild and precious life?

The question and the response are more significant than we imagine.

I see something long and arcing and multigenerational in the soul of the world. In this wilderness, forgiveness is like water. Our personal and familial wildernesses hold devastation and dark intent, but also solace and healing. The wilderness too, like the body of the beloved, is an essential home for the spirit.

As a boy with my father we'd prepare the fly rods and set out across a rancher's field until we made our way through bramble and brush to the edge of the water. We'd wade along the edge emerging below shallow rapids to watch the downdrift of the river. He'd find a smooth place from which to cast. That boy was grateful to be with him. Sun awash in the draw. The land a blend of timothy grass and cottonwoods along the river. Mountains before us. Mountains above and behind.

We stood not far apart, our bodies half in water—half dark, half light.

We were alive to each other.

The world was new again.

Dad

My dad grew up in a dust-blown town called Circle with a two-lane highway down the middle and dirt streets branching off the road like nondescript arms. Simple houses. Not much work other than ranching. He loved basketball. He hated school. Stubborn. Tough to work with, like a hard knot. So much so, his senior year the high school principal told him, "We're giving you a diploma you haven't earned." Calling him a hellion, the man said, "We don't want to have to deal with you for another year."

So he graduated, glad to be gone.

He worked roads in Montana. Grew from 5'8 to 6'4. Kept playing ball. City leagues. Independent tournaments. A couple of years later the road crew men told him he needed to go to college. Play some ball. He considered if he wanted to work roads the rest of his life. Though he despised school, he said he'd try again. He walked into the gym at Miles City Community College and found his way back to the coach's office.

"Hey, you got a scholarship for me?"

The coach didn't know him from Adam.

He looked up, saw my dad at 6'4, and said, "Yep, I do."

My dad struggled mightily his first year. Drinking and bar fighting along the way. He met my mom. He got better.

Student body president his second year. Better grades. Doing well in basketball. He went to Billings then, had a nice basketball career at Rocky Mountain College, earned a teaching degree, and went to Colstrip near the Northern Cheyenne reservation to teach and coach. He worked for the Department of Fish and Game for a while. He returned to school, earned a master's in teaching from Montana State University in Bozeman, and went to Alaska to teach and coach. More drinking and fighting. Tomcat. Nocturnal life. He returned to Montana, taught and coached at Plenty Coup on the Crow reservation. More alcohol. More fights. He and my mom divorced. Tough living. Loneliness. Father loss. Fear. A miraculous turn. He and my mom remarried. Then to St. Labre on the Northern Cheyenne reservation to be a principal and coach. Then to Livingston and Park High to coach my brother and me.

He learned. He failed. He loved. He stopped drinking.

Angry. He raised my brother and I to find our way.

Once my father was in the high country hunting big horn sheep in full winter when a blizzard set in and he came home. I thought he'd stay home for good measure. "Just getting a warmer sleeping bag," he said, and went back up the mountain.

Another time, I called from Washington and said, "What did you do this weekend?"

"Hunted lions," he said.

Among the most elusive animals in America, mountain lions have increased in population in Montana in recent years and the Montana Department of Fish, Wildlife and Parks has made more tags available. To hunt mountain lions, dogs are required. With other animals, generally a hunter goes out into the wilderness and spots the animal with binoculars or through a scope, and then secures a decent position in order to make a quality shot. This ensures a good chance of taking the animal. With mountain lions the dogs find the animal. My dad had a friend with some good dogs. He and his friend entered the mountains and when a fresh track was crossed the dogs followed the track until they treed the lion.

You can tell when the dogs find the trail by the bay of their voices.

You can tell by the dogs' barking when they have the animal treed.

When my dad approached, the lion was 80 feet up the tree.

He shot the lion with a bow.

The Family Who Lived with Their Faces to the Sky

A Septet

1/ THE BIG EMPTY

Skies run
from a tilted wood porch
all the way
to the horizon
and nothing keeps
back the dawn. Reservation cars, dirty white trucks,
people packed in yellow busses

carting fans to basketball games in midwinter,
sons of trappers
and daughters of sheep shearers,
the blood of a child
in the trunk of an Eldorado,
white crosses in twos or fives
at the bends of this two-lane mountain

are nearly transparent in the backlight.
Everyone here, remains.
People so insignificant they discover God
doesn't owe them anything.
In the deep high country
he is with his father. Grown men now.
A brother long gone.

Clouds surround the peak up high
to their right, forested at the base,
treeless and rocky at the top
where gold dark eagles fly in dawn's light.
South, the cloudbank thins
and sky reaches
from the ridge

where they stand and look out, down a draw
of scrub pine and mottled veins of sage,
blown timothy grass bent to the ground
and everything converging
along the silver-blue of the big river,
the sweep of the valley,
the four directions, the compass rose,

and far off a land mass: the broad back
of a giant sleeper. The wind comes from the north,
chill and fast from the gap of Canada
down from Glacier over the western mid-Montana plains
to the mountains again, the Beartooths,
the Bridgers, the Spanish Peaks, and blind northeast
behind them the Crazies, cerulean forms

of three plateaus and one high bulk of mountain,
gold mixed among the blue and in the valley shadow
the brown and tan of earth and grasses
bound to riverwater. The land takes them and holds them.
The land delivers them. The only son left alive
contemplates what he sees. You didn't owe us anything, he
        thinks,
but gave your own beloved.

2/THE HOUSE

He is nine, his brother eleven, summoned
to the relic zone,
their parents' bedroom,
where a mirror plate
trimmed in silver lies
set with their mother's rings
and lead crystal vials of perfume.

The boys sit together
on a blue flowered bedspread
tucked military sharp,
pillows encased and creased
with a hard feminine hand.
The femininity,
the absence of the masculine

surprises and hushes them
because they know the power
he has over her
and they feel deeply
the façade of this room,
the fear that holds her
here evenings into night

when he mans
the living room and watches TV,
or drives downtown
with alcohol to perform what he does
when he's gone, a silence
in the home that is physical.
Her dread engine.

She lies in the tight curve
of clean sheets and straight coverlet,
her boys breathing, sleeping down the hall.
They've heard her cry so often
they have no words. In that room,
in the afternoon light he is a big man.
Six foot four. Two hundred thirty pounds.

He holds his hands together,
presses his fingers to his forehead. Opens them
again. Bent face and body bent
inward, his shoulders round and chest caved,
his arms surround the cavity
he creates and his hands work the middle
like small animals.

He folds his arms finally,
stands over the boys and says,
Can't seem to make it work.
I'll be going now.
They cry.
He cries.
He leaves.

3/ THE FIRST DEFINITION OF PRETTY

He comes back
every other Tuesday night,
but ten minutes in she kicks him out,
screams, throws curses
like bombs
as her fists pound dents
in his down jacket.

She herds him
over the front steps,
along the front walk
to the driveway
as the boys watch
from the window
with their knees on the couch,

their bodies leaned
up the backrest.
Younger brother
touches nose to glass,
sees her face
blown out,
and white teeth shining,

feels
a release of bees
in his stomach
up under the ribcage.
Screen door black and grey,
the words from her mouth ugly,
and older brother

takes him by the hand
and walks him
to the kitchen.
When she returns
she gathers them in her arms
and sobs. Before now
they had never seen her

hit or cuss. Her husband
never did what she asked
either, but here they
watch him take
every punch like a man
made of glass.
He doesn't look at them

for fear of being
known for what
he is, but they witness
and each time they do they see
him go, and again older brother takes
younger brother's hand and they sit
at the kitchen table and wait.

4/THE FIRST DEFINITION OF UGLY

Every other Tuesday night. She doesn't attack anymore because he is a teacher and head coach at Plenty Coups, 35 miles south of Billings on the Crow reservation. Be respectable, she tells herself, but out there is where he introduces the boys to his girlfriend. That woman. How young? she asks, and the boys shrug. She looks white but she's mix, they say. She works with him. The games

are at the Shrine Gymnasium, small hot box thick with the smell of people and popcorn and the blond lacquer of hardwood. The players fly—Elias Pretty Horse, Tim Falls Down and Dana Goes Ahead—and they often win. At home at the oval oak table in the kitchen she sits with her hands folded over like meadow grass.

Is she prettier than me?

The boys race to answer. No, Mom. Never. Not even close.

I don't have to do what you say, the older brother says, and though they'd all thought these words countless times, he was the first to speak them aloud. This, four years after the father returned, left the young woman, remarried their mother. Either sublimation of sexual greed or a kind of family death wish in their father, either his brand of religion or just bad character made him more rigid than before. She cried in the back of the mobile home that arrived in two pieces on the flatbeds of 18-wheelers, a step up from the trailer at Bridger and the tiny apartment in Bozeman. The kitchen became the battleground. Younger brother's eighth grade year at St. Labre, school of Northern Cheyenne from Ashland, Lame Deer, and Busby, and Crow bussed in for the week from Lodge Grass

and Crow Agency. Late night a black rock, brick-sized, bashed through the window in his parents' room. Get down! The father yelled and the boy heard the wheels of a car getting gone, hard floor, open doorway, the father in the dark of the master bedroom shirtless in tight white underwear as he pointed a rifle out the window. Two months on, no sign of storm. In the house, a more intimate fight. Outside, bunchgrass stood white where the light

waned and far off a wound in the land revealed the crowns of cottonwoods in a narrow S naked of leaves above the Powder River, the water muddy brown even in late September. The father never hit the boys but for the familiar swing of the belt. Most often he ruled by volume and the clarity of brutal intention. The night sky nearly violet. The straight edge of the land framing a black void free of stars.

At the center line of the house grey carpet met worn linoleum. Different kitchen, same oak table, same wood chairs, older brother stood in the narrow space near the sink, his hands on a white Formica counter top embedded with gold-yellow grain like small truncated veins.   Younger brother left the kitchen, went to the cloth wingback in the living room and curled into the corner of the chair.   The door was closed, the windows shut.

5/THE FIRST DEFINITION OF FAMILY

Decrepit house crisp and clean,
the living room pungent with sweat,
younger brother cold watching
older in the fray
as if mauled
or made to fight
for air.
I'm not doing what you say!

Yes, I'm afraid
you are, the father says, eyes rocks
beneath his forehead
as the two approach,
more warships than men,
fists open.
No I won't, older brother says

and puts hands to the father's chest
and shoves him
back. The flush of neck and face.
The image of the father

throwing punches in bars, intoxicated
but intelligent, precise windmills that land
on the skulls of smaller men.

The father lifts the son
from the ground
and slams him
into the nearest oaken midback,
spins the boy to the window and
the purple sky over the cottonwoods splintered
by stars. Shut up, the father yells, and

when he clenches
the boy's white biceps, the boy's eyes go
wet, his face darkens,
his lips tremble.
No! the boy says firmly
but the first slap hits hard
and a white mark blossoms red,

wide, from the center of the cheek
over the cheekbone to the jaw line.
Shut up! the father says again,
I'm telling you.
No.

Skin twitch and body crimp, face swollen,
the son looks neither right nor left,

but stares into his father's eyes
while his mother leans
against the taupe-colored drapes
in the kitchen
and says, Please.
Shut up! the father shouts,
and she moves to the far side of the table

6/THE PEOPLE WITH THEIR FACES

and slips
into the living room,
the sheen
of her oldest boy's head,
the rooster flare
of her husband's face,
tears pinching the corners of her eyes
as her hands churn

and her mouth tastes like chalk.
Her husband beats the boy's face
for fifteen minutes straight.
The boy says No
and his father says Shut up
and takes full swings,
open-handed as a flatboard.

He dashes the boy's head
and hair to the side
until the boy,
close-mouthed
with a puffed, blotched face,
sits still
and doesn't cry anymore.

The boy
looks to
his father.
On the command,
Go to your room,
he rises
and walks

past his mother
and younger brother
like something fallen from the sky.
The image
of his shoulders,
the body burned
to hard white bone,

haunts the younger brother
through every wilderness.
The father
follows the boy
from the kitchen

to the end
of the mobile home

and they stay
in the back room.
If the older brother
says a word
the younger hears
nothing. Only wonders
if he is all right,

7/TO THE SKY

wishes for what
isn't there.
There is
no one,
just the island
of a solitary bed,
a grey ceiling, and loneliness.

The father
emerges, goes back
to the kitchen,
makes himself a sandwich
and drinks it down
with a glass
of water.

The older brother remains
face down on the bed,
and the next day
they return to their places:

the father
to his post
as principal,

the two brothers
to school,
their mother
to the linear enclosure
of the mobile home.
In a few short years
the older brother would be gone

into
the maw
of an ancient canyon,
his dark vehicle
burning
in open air
as it leapt the barrier

and fell
far into a valley
black with trees, where
the detonation
boomed and
the forest
bloomed with fire.

And for the rest
of their lives
the older brother spoke
to each one uniquely
tenderly.
His voice
immutable and holy.

The Burn We Carry

Reading a great short story is like walking a ridge in the Beartooth Range in southern Montana, perhaps on Two Rivers Plateau or the lip of the rock cirque above Hellroaring Lakes. You see the approach of a storm, a darkening above you that roils and moves, and suddenly you are struck by lightning. But you don't die, you live. The burn you carry with you for the rest of your life is the imprint of that story.

Some real imprints for me are "Father, Lover, Deadman, Dreamer" by Melanie Rae Thon, "Labors of the Heart" by Claire Davis, "Cry Cry Cry" by Sherman Alexie, "We Are Not In This Together" by William Kittredge, "Mudman" by Pinckney Benedict, "Lazarus" by Alan Heathcock, "Gold Star" by Siobhan Fallon, "Everything that Rises Must Converge" by Flannery O'Connor, "The Three Hermits" by Leo Tolstoy.

A novel is a lifetime of rivers and mountains, landslides and forest fires.

Oceans. Suns. Night skies. Stars.

A short story is lightning.

A river after rain. A swollen river. Violent. Peaceful.

A poem is like the breath we breathe.

A galaxy. A solar system.

A single wildflower.

Ladyslipper.

Shooting Star.

The breath of God.

Words like vessels to ferry the soul.

Stories and novels can be poems, and poems can be stories and novels, their cadence the call of Milosz from *The Witness of Poetry*:

> *What is poetry which does not save*
> *Nations and people?*

What the Jesuits call *the magis* is the idea that among many good things, the greater good should be discerned, and that *cura personalis*, or education of the whole person (heart, mind, and spirit) deepens the life of all humanity. Leadership is the study of personal, organizational, and global influence. In research on leadership and forgiveness studies the personal and the global meet: movements such as the Truth and Reconciliation Commission in South Africa, People Power 1 and 2 in the Philippines, the reconciliation ceremonies of the Nez Perce at the site of the Big Hole Massacre in northwest Montana, the ceremonies of the Cheyenne at the Sand Creek Massacre site in Colorado, and the Velvet Revolution from the Czech lands. The Lebanese writer Kahlil Gibran said the strong of soul forgive. A humbling statement, especially when I consider the enormity of the losses he records in his autobiographical book *The Broken Wings*.

I see a kind of spiraling pull from the externals of our personal lives down into the core of life, a natural desire in people to love and be loved. And yet tragedy is love's brother. In tragedy we can be completely undone. Our lives may enter an unforeseen and inscrutable darkness in which we are inconsolable even to the point of death. Yet in love, even in the crucible of our losses, there is often light. In that light we see one another as more exquisite than before.

I begin to comprehend how the body bears unaccounted trauma and becomes a nexus of multivalent fusion capable of complete healing, reconciliation, restoration, and atomically speaking, resurrection. The body can absorb pain and emit light. The mystery of the heavens, physical, present in us, hydrogen being the most abundant element in the universe, commonly referred to as the essence of light itself. Hydrogen is essential to life; it fuels the sun. Hydrogen is the element with the symbol H and the atomic number 1. Hydrogen is what powers the stars and comprises essential elements of our own DNA. Its most common isotope or form has one proton with one electron orbiting around it. A photon is a quantum of light (a discrete quantity of energy), created when a hydrogen atom absorbs energy/absorbs other photons, thus destroying those that are absorbed, and then emitting in turn, more photons. In numberless interactions throughout the universe a hydrogen atom absorbs another photon or two or three or more with the right energy to jump up to another energy level. After each of these "excitations" of the hydrogen atom, the electron could recede back down one or more steps, emitting photons along the way. If a photon with sufficiently large energy gets absorbed, this can even unbind an electron from its nucleus, a process called ionization. These crippled hydrogen atoms are no longer able to absorb or emit light. That is, until they manage to capture a free electron back into a bound energy level. When a hydrogen atom is crippled, it is only resurrected by this capturing process. In the atomic realm, this happens innumerable times per millisecond. In this sense, not just artistically but tangibly, the universe is both eternally dying and eternally resurrecting. As a poet, death awakens me, and life humbles me. Admittedly I have no real grasp of such mysteries. As Einstein said, "There are two ways to live your life. One is as though nothing is a miracle. The other is as though everything is a miracle. God is subtle but not malicious. The most beautiful thing we can experience is the mysterious—it is the source of all true art and science."

We are abandoned, but not only to loss, fear, and pain. We are also abandoned to pleasure, joy, and love. For me this fits with the nature of the destroying and resurrecting gone through by the essential elements of the universe and within our DNA. Who can say what truly gives us breath, what inspires? What carries us from holocaust and returns us to love? How I came to the notion of abandonment was through Rilke's *Book of Hours*. That and many years now as a researcher of genocide and forgiveness. At Gonzaga University, where I work as a professor of leadership and forgiveness studies, I watched a play based on the *Book of Hours* which primarily involved dance and other forms of powerful body movement multilayered below the words of Rilke. I love Rilke's work and feel graced to share his Czech heritage. He was born in Prague. My family is originally from Starý Plzenec, about an hour from Prague. I also feel a distinct difference between what I see as his vision of a beautiful God who abandons us, and my own questions regarding an intimate God who desires deeper and more authentic intimacy, more humane relations, and more devotion to the marginalized. I want to closely consider human responsibility, not blaming God (as we perceive God, however limited our understanding) for distance or harm, but recognizing we so often embody distance ourselves, and that perhaps we turn away from intimacy, human or Divine, because it is too much for us to bear. I have to acknowledge I am often incapable or too wounded to bear the numinous. Too crippled of heart or damaged of soul. I am in need of resurrection. Art considers the question of suffering. Beauty asks me to open inwardly into the possibility that it is not God who makes us suffer, who creates war, trauma, abuse, or bodily, emotional, mental, and spiritual harm, but rather it is we ourselves who harm and abandon each other.

To me, this is an even more devastating and largely inescapable reality: not God but us who abandon and harm the world, ecological and personal desperation being so pervasively and inescapably global.

I believe grief, depression, and fear, throughout the life span, are beloved others whose voices we ignore to our own peril. I love Carl Jung's image of drawing them near, drawing them close as you would a good sister to listen to what she whispers in your ear. The immensity of the losses we face are difficult to understand. Yet persistently, in terrible harms that range from genocide to the systematic abuses that occur in the life of the family, in my work as a clinical psychologist people open my soul again and again with the clarity and audacity of their heart for life. Here the

Divine in them and in the world resounds. Often when I returned home from my work when my daughters were young, one of them would ask me "Daddy, did you cry today?"

"Yes," I answered.

The simple beauty of the question overturns the atrocity in the world.

We are responsible to and moved by forces greater than ourselves. At the same time, we often evoke our own dignity or disgrace. I believe as men we borrow from the latent masculinity alive inside us, a place of shadow and fear that might in its self-shattering propensity also be referred to as the terrifying abyss of which the modern nuclear and environmental age speaks, the same terror to which the contemporary era of slavery, sex trafficking, atrocity and genocide is wed. The shadow, from Jungian psychology, is interwoven with the recurrent torque of an ancient truth that states the sins of the fathers are handed down to the third and the fourth generation. Jung's work is telling in this regard: in a true sense of mature intimacy, sex and feeling are unified, as are love and power as well as the feminine and the masculine. He said the more disembodied the shadow, the less spoken, the darker and denser it is, implying that in the disembodied man the will to exact punishment on self and others, both subliminal and overt, ascends like a mountain fire or drifts to an apathetic silence inhabited by those more dead than alive. In the sense of being alive to reality, acknowledging the darkness or evil that exists in us and others, we walk forward into an awareness not bound by cynicism or nihilism but confirmed in the loyalty that exists between the feminine and the masculine as well as between people, cultures, and nations.

The vastness of the wilderness in Montana and throughout the world finds equal magnitude in the vastness of the human heart. There is intimacy in the wilderness, and danger, just as there is intimacy and danger in our small towns, our cramped trailers, our homes, and sprawling cities. Are the invisible cities of Italo Calvino actually women and men and cultures? I believe such cities are the most lovely cities we know.

Hesperus

My four-year-old daughter handed me a card.
To Daddy written on the front
and inside a rough field
of five-pointed lights, and the words
You're my favorite Daddy in the stars.

In this western night we light the sky
like Vega, Deneb, Altair, Albireo,
the Summer Triangle,
Cygnus the Swan, our hair
tangled with wood and gravel,
our eyes like vacant docks
that beckon every boat.

Tell me about the word
stars, I said.

Oh, she said. Sorry.
I didn't know
how to spell world.

5.

Mountain Men

Mountain Men

A Triptych

1

In western Montana, the Rocky Mountain Front runs like a huge spine through the state. Often the mountains have a brooding temperament, filled with ferocity and storm. The eastern side of the state is enormous and mostly empty, a land of grass, horses, deer, and antelope. A silent, contemplative landscape. A state nearly 700 miles across that takes ten hours to drive, Montana is gigantic, haunting in splendor. The state contains no less than 100 mountain ranges: the Beartooths, the Crazies, the Absarokas, the Sapphires, the Beaverheads, the Sawtooths, and many more. Much of the landscape is made up of crags and ridges, cirques, spurs, and escarpments that touch the sky at 8,000 to 13,000 feet. All of Pennsylvania and much of the eastern seaboard of the United States can fit within Montana. When I think of the mountains of Montana, I think of gratitude, affection, humility. Yet Montana also hosts a history of Native American and Euro-American contact inscribed as much by atrocity and distance as dignity and desire.

The Beartooth Highway and the many trails and uncharted passages in the Beartooths are an invitation to a wilderness the like of which is found nowhere else. With vast plateaus at over 10,000 feet and more than twenty-five peaks over 12,000 feet, the land is blessed with uncommon immensity, difficult terrain, and alpine vistas in which you can find yourself both above and below the clouds. The scents are clean air and tree sap, musk and wildflower and scat. Steep granite mountains and ridges of crystalline metamorphic rock drop precipitously into valleys lush with forest, spanned by fields of grass, and touched with the silver of lakes and rivers, tributaries, and waterfalls. The land is home to grizzlies and black bears, mountain goats, bighorn sheep, elk, moose, mountain lions, wolves, wolverines, badgers, lynx, meadowlarks, red-winged blackbirds, red-tailed hawks, blue-capped tree swallows, gray owls, golden eagles, golden trout, brook trout, brown trout, cutthroat, and rainbows. A mountain lion can leap as high as 15 feet and as far as 40. A wolverine can cross nine mountain ranges in little more than a month of days. The Beartooths are seated on the vast Beartooth Plateau, the widest and most expansive true high elevation plateau in the United States.

In winter, the land is unpassable, and often deadly.

Steeped in obscurity until 1870 due to their remoteness, the valleys of the Beartooth Mountains were used by the Crow Nation for hunting and shelter from the blowing winds of the plains. Trappers entered the Beartooths in 1830 but U.S. Governmental expeditions did not occur until the late 1870s. Since that time nearly four-hundred species of plants have been found in the Beartooths, a mountain range considered the most biologically unique in North America. At over 9,000 feet, plants and grasses make their home above timberline, and below timberline the slant of the mountains is blanketed with spruce, fir, whitebark pine, and lodgepole.

I've grown to love the ways Montana's high country raised me.

Montanans grow up fishing, climbing mountains, wading rivers, playing basketball year-round, jumping off bridges, diving into cold clear water. And hunting. A man has rifles, his favorite rifles. For me, my father's old .22, the stock worn and darkened, good feel of wood in the hand, and a good line from gun to bird. Grouse, pheasants, sage hens, and wild turkeys end up fried hot or in a bubbling stew with potatoes and carrots and celery. For bigger animals, the Remington .243, again a gun of my father's, one he's had for forty years, lighter than most and with good range. Atop the rifle a wide-angle Redfield four-plex scope with a 2 to 7 power variable. The bullet travels 2900 to 3000 feet per second. Dinners of deer or elk steak, deer or elk hamburger, sausage made from the meat of the animal, along with excellent deer or elk jerky. Recently my father switched to a Smith and Wesson .22-250. The gun is lighter than the .243 but fires farther and faster, the bullet at 4000 feet per second. The gun is mounted with a Simmons 50 millimeter 3 to 9 power open face scope for larger field of vision. We shoot at 4 power. The mind and ear experience a reverse echo. You see the animal go down before you hear the report. The hide and rack of an elk are often sold to a fur buyer: the hide for 15 or 20 dollars, the complete skull and rack, raw, uncleaned, and frozen, for 60 or 70 dollars depending on size. The ivory teeth of a mature bull elk sell for 40 dollars a pair, and the ivory teeth of a mature cow elk sell for 10 dollars a pair.

The dark intensity and resplendence of the wilderness makes a home in you.

After middle school on the Northern Cheyenne reservation, we moved again and I went to high school in Livingston between the Crazy Mountains and the Beartooths, near the old entrance to Yellowstone National Park, an area that boasts peaks and valleys in abundance, the big river, a frontier of wildness and animals and relatively few people. Legend has it the Crazies are named for an insane woman who lived and died there. The Beartooths are upraised like teeth, and Beartooth Peak with its sharp predatory line defines the mountains. We didn't drag deer to the truck to be taken home and hung for the meat to cool and age. Instead we boned them out right in the field, which is more efficient for packing meat out of the high country. The process in detail is precise and involves leaving the bones and taking all the main areas for eating such as the backstraps and all four quarters, filets and cuts of meat from the neck and ribs, the elements that will feed you for the year. We skinned the animal and bagged the hide to trade it for a pair of leather gloves at the local hide and fur station. To quarter the animal, we cut through the shoulder and hip joints with the bone saw. We sawed off the hooves, throwing them aside. We placed the quarters, the rest of the meat, and the hide in black plastic garbage bags, tied the bags off and put them in our packs. If it was a trophy animal, we were careful to cape it out by taking the hide from the upper body, the area from the lower chest behind the front legs and up through the shoulders, neck, and head. We carefully sawed the head from the spine so head, horns, and cape could be packed out intact. If we didn't want to cape the animal but wanted the horns we simply sawed off the base of the horns connected to the skull plate over the brain. For a European mount the horns and complete skull are needed.

The skull is bleached white, the horns touched to natural brown, the skull and horns set on a wood backdrop. The look is stark and skeletal, and with the wide-tined tilt of a bull elk, stunning.

Our tools: the sharp narrow blade of the hunting knife, the thin sharpening cylinder, the small rectangle of the bone saw, and your own quickness and muscle. The body is fresh and hot so the skin comes off neatly as we turn the animal and move the knife along the skin-line where the white inner lining separates from the fat and muscle of the body. If we are in bear country, we work fast to limit the amount of time the scent of fresh meat is in the air. In our absence the remains of the animal feed bears, wolves, and hawks, as well as coyotes, crows, and other scavengers. In the end the body is picked clean by animals and insects and the bones go dry and white from exposure to sun, wind, rain, and snow. For years when I walk that same path, I see those bones, and I remember.

As a high school teacher in Montana, my dad wasn't paid well so we lived on deer and elk. Birds, some antelope. With the big animals, we brought the meat back home and cut it into steaks, which we wrapped in butcher paper and marked and put in the freezer. The rest we took to a local shop to be made into hamburger, sausage, and jerky. With birds, we snapped the neck, then cut and peeled back the skin before we bagged them and took them home.

Though we lived in town, the towns were small. Mom grew up in a town of eight people. Her dad had a ranch and also drove wheat or livestock for other ranches. In that wide empty landscape the town also had a community school. My father's father sheared sheep and worked various odd jobs. His mother waitressed at the local diner.

Marvels of landscape. Marvels with regard to people. My mother raised a grand prize winning heifer. My father tried bull riding just to say he did. My grandma loved watching a good cutting horse, light in the foot, horse and rider in a unified dance. Ranching, hunting, livestock, horses, cutting horses, rodeos, bronc riding, team roping, steer wrestling. Wilderness. Home.

On the Blackfeet reservation in Browning on the northern highline just off the east side of Glacier, almost everyone has horses. When I was there not long ago, a couple of high school students rode their horses down the town's single main street. I watched as they took the horses through the Subway drive-through, picked up lunch, and rode on. The small towns, and every Montana town is a small town, are known for isolation, love, and loneliness, people at times fully alive or sold to pain, a lot of drinking, high rates of unemployment, economic and emotional despair, suicide, and violence, as well as strong families, humility, humor, respect, courage.

In eastern Montana my dad grew up poor, lanky, and in love with hunting and basketball.

While teaching and coaching high school teams, it took a long time before he scrambled out of the spiral of alcohol. Over the years I grew up in a couple of different trailers and one mobile home. Huge animal heads lined the walls and took up half the open space. You'd have to walk around those animals with their large shoulders and narrow heads that bore huge racks of horns. They were all mounted on the walls, nosing their way into the living room.

Now my parents have a house that overlooks the gap toward Livingston, the Bridgers and the Spanish Peaks. When you come into the great room, high walls lead to a ship's prow of twenty-foot windows. Those heads still stare you down. To the right as you enter you see a pair of mountain goats as well as a stone sheep and a dahl sheep with horns on a full curl. Above your head behind you is the head of a bear, wide mouth bearing teeth. To the left you find the head of a caribou, two antelope, a very large elk, a whitetail buck, a mule deer buck, and down on the floor a full-length mountain lion. All this put terror in me as a child whenever I walked through the trailer at night. The wonder of it still strikes me.

2

Home, or the loss of it, reverberates in the people and cultures of the American West. Sometimes downplayed or subdued, most often revealed as wrecked or shattered, the sense of subliminal grief is pervasive and painful and raises questions about the wilderness we call family, about women, and about men.

'When my father turned 70 he said, "I guess the Lord saw fit to bless me," and it wasn't the 70 years he was talking about. It was the wilderness. This season my father brought home two turkeys, an elk, two deer, two antelope, and a mountain goat, feeding a veritable passel of people including an older couple who advertised on Craig's List wanting venison. The mountain goat he found in the Crazies, a hunt he took alone in the high country, cresting plateaus, rock walls and jagged shale slides a thousand feet above the tree line. He went farther than expected in order to approach the billy from above.

He shot the animal behind the shoulder on a steep slant from 300 feet. The mountain goat collapsed and slid down a narrow chute, and it took time and caution for my father to reach the place where the animal came to rest on a razor uplift of rock. There he straddled a rock spine, standing over an expanse of sky, and boned out the animal. He knew he would need to work fast. In a pathless place, being caught coming down the mountain after dark is not pleasant. In his precarious position above the clouds, a job that normally takes him 45 minutes took over two hours. With his hunting knife and bone saw he quartered the animal, removed the meat, cut off and discarded the hooves, and took the cape, head, hide and horns. Finally, the sun leaning toward last light, the heavy pack was ready and he began his descent. Just after dusk he emerged on the flat below the mountains, made his way to his truck, and returned home.

For years my father and I could not express our weaknesses to one another. Nor could we easily express our kindness. I gained his love for basketball and went from battles against Jonathan Takes Enemy, to battles on the streets of L.A., to battles in gyms all over the country on the road to March Madness. With pro ball in Germany I faced foes in Berlin, Wolfenbüttel, Bamberg, Leverkusen. Home, I'd face my dad and wonder if we knew each other at all, wonder if the deep-seated bitterness that seemed to reside in me like a thorn could be removed. Of conflict, we didn't talk much. Or if we did, it seemed he raged while I grew silent. We entered the East Gallatin and set down dry flies over clear water. We didn't speak our faults. Our great lacks, and separate hungers. We concealed them in our bodies. We released them on each other. Still, we lay on our backs beneath cottonwoods on the flats below the Crazies before dawn and waited for wild turkeys to come visible in the trees. And still, his hand on my shoulder steadied me before I focused the scope on a whitetail buck whose crown was barely visible above the grass.

In those years, battles could be hot and full of wrath and mostly irresolvable, but in later life, by subtle turns love came to us, and taught us about forgiveness. It started when my wife spoke quietly to me in bed after dark in my parents' house. "Tell him you love him," she said. "Don't wait. Put your arm around him. Touch him."

"Why?"

"Because," she said. I want you to be a man who can touch. I want you to be a man who can give love to his father."

A burn entered my chest like a dry August fire, like trees ravenously consumed.

"Go to him," she said.

"And do what?" I questioned.

"Apologize. Ask his forgiveness."

"Definitely not," I said.

She looked at me, closely. She waited, and over the years she won me over. I began to listen. What she asked I tried to do, haltingly for a very long time, before things opened up and kindness presented itself more readily between my father and me. The physical landscape of Montana as well as the interior landscapes of people give a small glimpse into the reality of how we ask for and receive forgiveness, and how we navigate atonement. The land in its expressions of time and weather and seasons, mirrors how we change, and how we love. The soul of the wilderness is the soul of the world of which Teilhard de Chardin speaks— "driven by the forces of love, the fragments of the world seek each other so that the world may come to being. In each soul, God loves and partly saves the whole world which that soul sums up in an incommunicable and particular way."

In America there is presently so much grief and loss between races, between women and men, and specifically between men and men. In a harsh, long season of winter, spring can seem a distant dream. In the context of cold or hardened relationships, health or communion can be hard to fathom. Many men do not have words for their relationship to women or to other men. Here, when combined with a wordless or muted interior, the Montana landscape evokes an even more isolate and rugged exterior, often gesturing to the stylistic characteristics of each man's own physicality. A man's generational family line, his temperament, his response to abuse or violence or vacancy is embedded in a Western landscape as bleak as it is arresting, as fatal as it is filled with life.

My father's hands, like my own, contain large crevices, dislocated joints, oversized knuckles, cuts, scars, spots, discolorations. They are familiar with wood and rock, metal and water. They contain large distances. They do not lend themselves naturally to softness.

For a man who cannot find words to express feelings the result is often a potent bend toward that which is distant and apathetic or harsh and desolate, violent, even deadly.

Such men tend to live emotionally silent or physically loud and largely defunct familial lives. In a dense shadow of their true selves they shun relational engagement by living in apathy or aggression toward that which is lovely in others. They are empty and void, and they are experienced as meaningless or incapable of generating meaning. By violence or apathy, men cut off the feminine and succeed in harming their relationships with women and other men. Even if it is a known truism that all men benefit from a healthy balance of the feminine and the masculine, many men find it very difficult to hold respect for the feminine within their own masculinity. Interwoven dualities such as resolve and gentleness, love and power, justice and mercy, and transparency and boundary are necessary for the feminine and the masculine to relate on an in-depth level. To the meaningless man a healthy balance of such qualities is beyond him.

In the inner world his impact is often graceless. Broken relationships, fractured families, the border of despondency, the fall from grace. Men who reject grace or lack grace can be stubborn, hard as concrete. It is as if they have left a sense of home behind. I've alienated myself in the same way. At the same time, a desire to return exists in the core of the masculine and in the men of the American West. My father, after all these years, rises from his chair when I make the seven-hour journey to his house. "Welcome home," he says. He comes to me and holds me in his arms. He kisses my cheek. In my experience, men yearn for oneness with others. Yet without atonement a life of unyielding consequence tracks us, often in predatory fashion.

3

Consider the Sand Creek Massacre. Consider the Big Hole Massacre. Consider the massacre at Lidice. Like individual men, dominant culture bears the wound of its own moral shadow—its own proclivity for evil—and from such wounding, collapses inward and destroys itself and everyone it touches. Without atonement, individual men never recover their humanity; they merely echo the desolate voice of the dominant culture that holds them captive.

Even so, the mystery of life and the hope for love is irrevocable, felt even in men whose interiority can often appear more mountain-like than human. Cold, massive in darkness or density, far removed from the intimacies of daily life, such men suffer. The mountains are home to so much, I like to think men can give that sense of home to the loved ones around them. Experiencing the mountains not as distant, but close to the heart, has shown me men crave something higher. When you enter the wilderness, you know the awe and fear wilderness commands, and at the same time you know the intimacy wilderness imparts without measure. In a similar way, for men who desire a pathway home, when they find a way to set out on this path, they traverse the landscape bravely and with endurance.

Kierkegaard said purity of heart is to will one thing.

Home is a place of peace, reunion, and reconciliation, where love, discernment, and wisdom reside. Home, rather than dislocation or displacement. That home could be the sacredness of Native American traditions in Montana such as those of the Tsitsistas (Northern Cheyenne) or the Niitsítapi (Blackfeet) or the Ochethi Sakowiŋ (Sioux), or it could be a sense of home which heralds from a far homeland such as my own Czech and German heritage. Home is found in America, in the blood of the America we hope in and for which we openly seek a healing that will reverse the descent of the present and lead us to the reality of a more responsible future. Home is acknowledged or embraced, challenged, attacked, or divided as a result of the level of privilege we have or the level of atrocity we have suffered in our families, nationally, or culturally.

Home is found in the wilderness that surrounds us and the wilderness within us.

Notably, emotional and spiritual wilderness can be as treacherous as physical wilderness. In the mix of Native American and Euro-American culture in Montana and in the American West, imaginative and essential life comes of honoring cultures while also directly facing the atrocities of the present and the past. Of ultimate value is an authentic naming of the atrocities and massacres, the overt and covert harms, the pervasive human rights abuses as well as the reconciliations that have transpired in Montana history and in American history as a whole. In the concept of home and the lived experience of home, the masculine is often an unconscious weapon that is violently projected, rather than something that is contemplative, established in dignity and received with dignity. Listening is diminished or destroyed. The healing of the masculine involves receiving the influence of the feminine, of home, and of the will to be honorable, intimate, and life-giving in the center of culture and country.

When I think of Montana, a place as fraught with race and gender discrimination as any place in America, I wonder what can lead us deep into the wilderness of atonement and return us to one another. I picture my father walking through dusk, the animal strapped to his back, the cape and horns catching light.

I picture Cleveland Highwalker walking beside him.

When my father comes home from the mountains and gives to us from what he's been given, we receive him with open arms. We greet him with gratitude for how he went at 70 into the heights of a rough and relentless country. We eat well, and celebrate how good it is to be alive and wild.

We gaze with open eyes on the wilderness of this world.

I'll Fight Until I Die

"Take a look at that," my dad says, sliding the newspaper across the kitchen table. Usually when he does this he's referring to a goring in Yellowstone National Park or in one of the nearby mountain ranges, places made equally of grandeur and fear. I recall an incident that involved a tourist who left her car to get a closer look at a bull moose. The moose approached with a wide spoon rack and put the front tine through her eye, pinning her to the door. She did not survive. On this journey home, the story he shows me on the front page of the Bozeman *Daily Chronicle* is of particular interest.

As sometimes happens in remote areas, a man had quit the rat race and taken to the wilderness. He'd been out two years, known to local ranchers and farmers, living a hermit life, a mountain man existence. On a given day high up in the Beartooth Range, he was low to the ground as he inspected some vegetation. When he lifted his eyes a mother grizzly stared him full in the face. In a moment she was on top of him.

Normally in stories like this the bear kills the man. But this time the man did not try to run or play dead, he grew aggressive. He raked and clawed and became animal himself. Almost like a death wish such a response is not one a grizzly, let alone a mother grizzly backs away from. Normally the bear makes quick work of the man. But this time it was different. In the man's aggression he scrambled, reached from the bear's chest upward and dug his nails into the soft flesh of nose, where he raked fiercely downward.

The bear barked and ran away.

In the heart of the wilderness there are mysteries.

The man stood, his head pierced and gashed, blood running from his wounds.

He made it to his truck two miles away.

He drove to the nearest ranch house and knocked on the door.

A woman answered.

"We need to get you to the hospital," she said.

"I'm not going to any hospital," he responded.

"You're going to the hospital right now!"

She wrapped his face and head in a towel, directed him to her car and drove him to town.

The picture on the front page of the *Chronicle* shows the man seated on the edge of a hospital bed, his shoulders slumped, a taciturn look on his face. His head is balding. His face and the dome of his skull are laced with more than a thousand stitches.

A reporter interviewed him.

"Most people are killed in a confrontation of that kind. What were you thinking when the bear was on top of you?"

Hard-faced, close-mouthed, the man was quiet for some time.

"I'll fight until I die," he said. "That's what I thought."

I put the paper down. My head was sweating.

The fortitude of people.

I see this same will when I read Francis Winwar's *The Immortal Lovers*, about Elizabeth Barrett Browning and Robert Browning, or Diane Wood Middlebrook's evocative work on the life of Anne Sexton, or N. Scott Momaday's *House Made of Dawn*, Toni Morrison's *Home*, or Arthur Miller's violent play *The Crucible*.

Narrative is the place in the literary arts where poetry and prose intersect. At this crossroads there is hope, even in the global uncertainty that inhabits people and nations. We reunite with people at the crossroads. We go from there together. Reading, writing, seeing others with new eyes, is a journey that reminds us of the subtle presence of empathy in the world, a journey of darkness and light in which after we have lost one another we find each other again.

Vincent Van Gogh said, "There is nothing more truly artistic than to love people." Such love brings about justice and engenders grace. My wife has taught me the artistry involved in truly loving and serving others is imbued with authentic power. In the artists I look to for direction—from former Montana Poet Laureate Sandra Alcosser to Blackfeet Gros Ventre writer James Welch, from the Dutch painter van Gogh to the German composer Johann Sebastian Bach, from Alice Walker of the American south to Marilynne Robinson of the American Midwest and West—such power helps heal us of our individual and collective wounds.

Yes tragedy and atrocity bruise the world with unabated disorder.

Yet genuine power is often ferocious, often tender.

I am reminded of the heart of that mountain man.

I'll fight until I die.

Great art is given to that elemental heart, full of fury and fire. A place where we are shaped and influenced to choose the paths we choose. From my first engagements with people who gave me love, I found decent women and men shaped by forces beyond them as well as by their own sense of humility and determination.

I think of childhood in Alaska: silver salmon runs, crabs at war on flat rocks, crabs that clamp with powerful pinchers and remove each other's arms, rain like a kiss that touches your face on hikes in the mountains above Sitka, a singlewide trailer kept clean, rocky beaches along the coast, guitar songs and driftwood and glass tumbled by the world's ocean, and Mom and Dad caught in some hard pain, weary to the bones.

I think of childhood in Montana: music like silver leaves falling in the house, dancing to the Imperials, running like a banshee in Hershey's track meets and losing, throwing a softball for distance and winning, the early love of basketball, Max Spotted Bear, Tim Falls Down, Dana Goes Ahead, and Marty Round Face—the Crow Nation, increasingly hard-knotted pain in Dad and Mom and within them the alcohol, the infidelity, the desperation, the raft of the human soul over the lip of the abyss and down into the dark.

From Montana, I remember the difficult terrain forged of the death of my parents' marriage, ugliness, alienation, divorce, then the silver ring of forgiveness forged of my parents' re-marriage to one another, more love and life and basketball, music and wilderness, rivers, sky, stars and

172

wonder, more pain, anguish, fragileness and brokenness. Desecration and self-hate, hubris and humility, good-hearted people with interior imbalance like the edge of a landslide, a two-shafted mobile home stitched together at the mid-line, basketball like a waking dream, Cleveland Highwalker, Lafe Haugen, Russell Tall White Man, Richard Little Foot, Blake Walks Nice, Elton Killsnight—the People, the Cheyenne, the Tsitsistas; to Livingston and Paradise Valley in the heart of the Rockies and a singlewide trailer with a green skirt, and two State titles and dunk city, and basketball for Montana State University with my brother, Pepperdine, and then pro ball in Germany shooting deep jumpers and rising up and throwing down, and the release from there, out into marriage to my wife Jennifer, a musician who is one with the elements: namely fire.

Power in the hand, and love in the body.

She and I working in the mines of marriage.

Pain and self-absorption and hard living and dark words.

Liberated finally into friendship. The enduring submission to wise mentors.

Married like fools in love, still in love decades later.

And I think of life as a husband and father: the mystery of consolation and desolation, quiet night hours of silence and poetry and prose, listening to the vital pulse of so many writers, musicians, composers, artists, memorizing sacred texts, musical compositions, lines of plays, poems, stories, more basketball, and more of the beloved grace of being married to Jennifer, the woman who has my soul forever, and the cherished gravity of being the father of Natalya, Ariana, and Isabella.

What is worth fighting for?

Jennifer and our three girls are perhaps best described by their dance styles on family dance night when we break out in collective joy. Someone starts it and we turn up the volume and let go and the living room becomes precisely the place where Jennifer dances like a wild celestial being, Natalya becomes deerlike, performing her own ghostly movement, Ariana loves the soul of ballet and takes flight, and Isabella dances like a whirlwind.

Our daughters share the same middle name, Alexis, given by their mother.

Alexis means defender of mankind.

Thankfulness is hard to come by, and perhaps impossible to live without.

A joyful heart is like a medicine, the proverb says, a broken spirit dries the bones.

When I think of family, I tell myself I'll fight until I die.

I looked up from the table after reading the article about the mountain man.

"What do you think?" my Dad asked.

"I don't know if I have that kind of courage," I said.

He tipped his head down. "None of us know," he said, "until the moment comes."

He looked at me then, tenderly.

In the heart of life, we fight until we die.

And when we die, I believe we go deeper into love.

I Want to Ask Your Forgiveness

My wife Jennifer and I were in our early twenties, not yet married. I was at the dinner table with her and her family when her father said something short, a sharp-edged comment to her mother. At the time Jenn's father, Fred, was the president of a multi-national sports corporation based in Washington state. Thinking back, I hardly noticed the comment, probably due to the chaos and uncontrolled ways I had often experienced conflict in the past. For me, most conflicts meant flashes of force followed by a simmering resentment that went underground, plaguing the relationship, taking a long time to disperse. On a 100-point scale of verbal violence, for me his exchange with his wife, Susie, would have been a minus 8 or so. I did not give her father's comment a second thought until sometime after dinner when he approached me as I relaxed on the couch. He had just finished speaking with his wife over to one side of the kitchen when he came to me.

"I want to ask your forgiveness," he said, "for when I was rude to Susie."

I could not imagine what he was talking about. I felt uncomfortable, and I wanted to get him and me out of this awkward conversation as soon as I could. From there the tension only increased for me. I had not often been in such situations in which things were handled in an equitable way.

My work experience had been that the person in power (typically, but not always, the male) dominated the conflict so that the external power remained in the dominant one's hands, while internally everyone else (those not in power) suffered bitterness, disappointment, and a despairing nearly hopeless feeling regarding the good of the relationship. Later in my family and work relationships I found that when I lived from my own inordinate sense of power, I too, like those I had overpowered, would have a sick feeling internally for having won my position through coercion rather than through the work of a just and mutual way of being. In the situation with Jennifer's father, I felt tense and wanted to quickly end the moment by saving face for both of us.

"You don't have to ask me," I said.

"I don't ask forgiveness for your benefit," he responded. "I ask to honor the relationship I share with my wife. In our family, if one person hurts another, we not only ask forgiveness of the person who has been hurt, but also of anyone else who was present in order to restore the dignity of the one we've hurt."

From a relatively brief experience, I gained respect for myself and began see the possibilities of an artistic way of life free of perpetual binds and rifts, and free of the entrenched criticalness that usually accompanies such relationships. My own life was like a fortress compared to the open lifestyle Jennifer's father espoused. I began to understand that much of my self-protection, defensiveness, and lack of will to reveal myself might continue to serve as a fortification when in future conflicts, but would not lead me to more whole ways of experiencing the world.

The mature atheist believer understands kindness while the hard believer atheist has contempt and below contempt cruelty. I see these categories not so much as binaries but a continuum or mosaic that exists in each of us, in our individual and collective humanity and inhumanity, forming a spiral or quantum dynamic. The more rigidly defined I am, the more contempt and cruelty I express, whether my affections be atheist or theist; equally, the more loose or undefined I am, the less cohesion toward moral or intimate responsibilities to myself and others, let alone toward enemies. Who can claim to know the nature of the sacred or the profane in ourselves or in the universe? Some of my favorite atheists are among the most kind people I know, others are among the most toxic and wasteful of humanity; likewise, some of the most religious or spiritual people I've encountered are among the most giving and self-sacrificial, and others are among the most deranged and ill-formed in both intention and impact. I find this easily proven with even a cursory look at human history and daily life. Of course, in a more humane sense, all of us are, I believe, comprised of both good and evil; hard to measure, even more difficult to predict.

So for me, it is not religion or atheism or other epistemologies that are the problem with humanity, it is our unimaginable capacity for hypocrisy, for lying to ourselves and others in order to enact self-preservation and other-deprivation; and it is not atheism or spirituality that truly define our capacity for collective humanity, but rather the grace and mercy to transcend ourselves in order to love and serve others. For me, I humbly hope in what my mother tried to teach me when I was a boy: the simple, profound understanding that God is love. In the context of living a life attuned to both art and science, I've found atomic theory is a nearly unlimited space of discovery and imagination. Max Born's original text details the nature of the stars in scientific terms, as well as the finest granules of the substructure of atoms, and in the end, he points in his final sentence toward the notion that no one can fully know the mystery of life. Fission and fusion are interdependent in many ways, fracture and unity. I love the juxtaposition of the science of atomic theory with the art of intimacy, how fracture and union play out in the stellar expanse, locally, in our bodies atomically and subatomically, and in the touch I experience when my wife or daughters hold my hand.

Jennifer's father shed crucial light on my understanding of conflict. Light, being quantum, symbolizes ultimate forgiveness, ultimate fusion, and ultimate love. Light honors what Isaiah referred to as "the garment of praise instead of the spirit of despair." In this light, life asks us to humble ourselves and to honor relationships with others as infinitely worthy of mutual care. In Greenleaf's terms, this takes the form of listening and understanding, and only the one who seeks to honor the inherent worth of other human beings is able to approach people first by listening and trying to understand, rather than by needing to be understood. The artist expresses the unique grandeur of the beloved other through consolation, desolation, and persuasion, rather than approaching art through coercion, manipulation, or brute force. As Greenleaf noted, just as "true listening builds strength in other people," it follows that a lack of listening weakens people and weakens artistic viability.

In basketball, to listen is to evoke chemistry, teamwork, unity, and victory. As teammates we honor each other in a collective engagement involving risk, responsibility, cost, and opportunity. And now that my life has entered a place where the discipline of basketball gives way to the discipline of poetry, I wonder again what it means to truly listen. When reading a great poem, for example, we touch the face of the beloved through the heart and soul of the artist. A covenant with humanity is formed that is both timeless and immanent. A covenant of mind and body, a covenant of spirit in which physical wilderness grounds me: trillium, deer's-head, orchid, fawn lily, the face of a child or the skeleton of an elk, bone-fanned after a few winters, the unknowable expanse of night, the light of morning. The human wilderness is no less concrete: my will to subdue others, their will to subdue me. Our collective will to transcend ourselves into greater love. I want to assume a bodily posture of humility, giving deference to the quietly pervasive silence, or what some refer to as the voice of God, however we may comprehend the incomprehensible. The Divine is an unfathomed essence, and at the same time an embodied care, peace, strength, and kindness. When I consider atomic realities in the universe they seem just the right form of infinite to give me comfort. I want to hold these and be held by them. I want to see others held and beheld. For me, the sacredness of this holding occurs when my wife and I sit together at the kitchen table. She reads to me. Or I read to her. We read aloud. Or when we lie down together at day's end and enter the night like stewards of one another's well-being.

At night we more fully enter the shadow.

The shadow might be captured, if obliquely, in the symbol of Ursus Arctos Horribilus: the North American brown bear, or grizzly. When I consider bears, I'm reminded of the naturalist Doug Peacock, a friend to many, and a man who has spent much of his life in the company of grizzlies. He reminds me that wilderness may be the only thing that can save us from ourselves. When we preserve wilderness, we preserve the beauty of nature and grace against the atrocities of industry, consumerism, and greed. In wilderness, perhaps even more so at night, we recognize the need for humility in the face of fate. Peacock echoes the clarion call of Edward Abby who stated that global warming and human activity equal extinction. In the face of unknowable risks and a largely uncertain future, Peacock calls me to the kind of listening that results in awareness and action. In his years in the mountains in the presence of an animal that can take human life with the sweep of an arm, Doug's vision carries us.

"Humility, he said, "is the emotional posture behind reason."

What does it mean to listen to art, to the artists of our nation and our world? What does it mean to listen to Elizabeth Alexander, Charlotte and Emily Brontë, the Kokinshū, Sappho, Tolstoy, Natalie Diaz, Layli Long Soldier and all who commandeer the vessels of our dreams? My wife is selfless, graceful, spiritually formidable, and beloved. Most often at night, I write poems in conversation with her, even when she sleeps. Her uniquely infinite self in communion with me, hand in hand, her dignity and power. After all we've been through, after everything the human family has endured, generation to generation, I feel such abiding grace. Poems emerge from that silence and are kept quietly between her and me for a very long time. In many ways, I think quietness attends all of us, meeting us intimately, enjoining a mutuality we did not foresee. Night silence is an image of God to me, more cadenced, melodic, and vocal than I imagined. The wilderness of the universe shows the deepest things are not fully knowable in a finite sense. But not knowing is a gift. In the same way that we can never fully know a loved one, the unanticipated abundance of the Great Mystery is essential to our oneness.

Writing late at night in the half dark of the house, a light opens the dark and helps me seek.

The question drives me deeper into life.

6.

Of Sunlight

Going to the Sun Road

Growing up in Montana, and having experienced the darkness of Montana winters, I tend to seek a certain light. At sunrise over East Rosebud Lake, or sunset in the Crazies, the light gives such clarity I wonder at the sheer scale of the wilderness and the largesse of existence. The sky appears more spacious and more intimate, and people an intricate part of the interplay between darkness and light.

Years back in the graduate writing classes I took, however, this light-bearing quality was readily dismissed: the world was inanimate matter, singularly immovable, and people bit-actors in a cosmic play that had no design and no playwright. Most of my professors referred to the landscape of the American West as devoid of interrelation, agency or animation, calling the land "indifferent" or "coldly removed." People were killed by the weather, or by the work it took to survive. In this stark rendering of wilderness, people often took their own life or the lives of others, suiciding under the weight of loneliness the West evoked, or harming their neighbors, crazed by the hardness of a desolate landscape.

Each time the conversation went in this direction in a poetry or fiction class, my discomfort was twofold: one, my personal experience of the wilderness was anything but indifferent, and two, the analysis was too reductionistic for my taste, lacking any notion of the primarily unified or fractured relationship between landscape and people. My own experience of the wilderness had often surprised me with just how loving and how hateful it could be. I believe the wilderness, steeped in the numinous, makes demands of us. I remember when I nearly drowned in the Yellowstone River after being beaten against the rocks on a day as filled with sunlight and beauty as any I'd seen. I recall our family's hunting dog walking a tight circle around her body on a bed of pine needles. She took nearly twenty minutes in a rainstorm so torrential we couldn't see the lake only a few feet beyond the trees. Finally, she lay down, placed her nose on her paws and slept a deep, peaceful sleep. Mystic Lake darkening through the trees. I saw forked lightning on black skies, and when the clouds cleared a glow of sun that made everything glisten. In northwest Montana, Going to the Sun Road rises from a river valley straight to the top of the mountains. The peaks are sharp and massive, black rock skirted by forest. In early July, you see hillsides with beargrass like pale torches, meadows cloaked in paintbrush and lupine, fireweed and glacier lily.

Further down, devil's club pierces the forest floor.

The Blackfeet named the mountains there the Backbone of the World.

My father was raised by men who were hunters and trappers, so my brother and I share a strange inner world familiar with skull and horn, the eye teeth of elk, bear claws, the jawbones of small animals, a magpie's tail feathers, the notch of color at the shoulder of a red-winged blackbird. When we moved from Billings to the far southeast corner of Montana to live on the Cheyenne reservation, I learned three symbiotic truths: that fear exists in great measure, in me and others; that wilderness is not indifferent but something beloved, like a sister or brother; and that people who lack decency live alongside those of uncommon dignity all across America. During the Indian Wars the Cheyenne were called the Beautiful People. Their leadership structure consisted of 44 chiefs, with 4 chiefs above 40. Leaders were chosen based on their ability to serve the people. I think again of the Sand Creek Massacre of 1864 when Cheyenne women, children and elders were executed by Colonel John Chivington and his troops. Chief Black Kettle survived. His wife was shot nine times, and she too survived. From that point forward she was called Woman Hereafter.

After the massacre Chief Leg-in-the-Water said, "What do we want to live for? The white man has taken our country and killed all our game. He was not satisfied with that but killed our wives and children. Now no peace. We want to go and meet our families in the spirit land. We loved the whites until we found out they lied to us and robbed us of what we had. We have raised the battle axe until death."

So the Cheyenne warred against the whites, joining Lakota and Arapaho warriors, ambushing U.S. military and Infantry in the Fetterman Fight, leaving not one alive. They cut the limbs from those bodies in vengeance over Sand Creek. Again, the Cheyenne succeeded with the Lakota and Arapaho at the Battle of the Greasy Grass (the Little Big Horn), piercing Yellow Hair Custer until he died, killing every man in the five companies under his command.

On the reservation my brother and I were white as chalk among three hundred Cheyenne and Crow students in the K-12 school we attended. I felt afraid most of each day for about the first year. It wasn't until I "earned" some nicknames that I started to feel more at ease.

Casper the Friendly Ghost, for example.

"What's up Casper? How's life as a ghost these days?"

My best friend Lafe Haugen, Cheyenne and a marvelous basketball player, smiled and made me feel welcome. Looking back, I know he protected me quite a bit. He was the toughest in our class and also the funniest in a place known for quick humor. When we came into the room, the older ones nodded at us with their noses, saying, "Here comes Salt and Pepper." We played basketball every recess, every lunch hour, and every day after school until long after dark. On the court at night we mixed with grown men and it felt like danger. It was some of the finest basketball I've ever been a part of, including my years as a Division 1 player, and in Germany as a professional. Reservations are proving grounds. I was called "honkey" or "white boy" more times than I care to remember.

My father prided himself on being a strict disciplinarian. He could be fun, even exceptionally funny with his friends, but as the high school principal he was as flexible as a concrete wall. Big and imposing, his leadership was a daunting and personal militarism. His nickname among the student body: "Ayatollah Khomeini." They said it aloud, naming him after the Supreme Leader of Iran who was accused of being a dictator by his enemies and who haunted American news coverage for some time. My father loved the nickname, even took pride in it, smiling at it over dinner, laughing. Cheyenne humor is often direct with multiple layers of resounding irony. But Cheyenne life can also be violent. Not surprisingly, one morning my father found his office window shattered, and a bullet embedded in the wall near the door.

If, as in ancient Christian mysticism, dust returns to dust and the earth is the body, then topography can be grace, and wilderness, love. Of course, this distinction the soul attains by going through fire: by engaging the crucible with dignity, by giving and receiving mercy, and by transcending one's own ego on behalf of others—in effect, by abandoning the self, one gains greater life with the beloved. In like fashion Montana wilderness is a place daunting and challenging not only physically or geographically, but emotionally, mentally, and spiritually, even as it harbors undeniable good.

Of significant note in Montana is the painful history between Catholic culture and traditional Cheyenne culture, and paradoxically, the complex and sinewy relationship they still share. What I remember most about the Cheyenne reservation was not the danger or fear or the way my own skin seemed as thin as the windows in our mobile home. What I remember most is the love my family received, wholehearted and prevailing, despite America's genocidal history and the entrenched inequities of the present day. Not just from Lafe Haugen and his family or Cleveland Bement and his, but from many families. Basketball was brotherhood, and life was filled with hilarity and friendship. Cheyenne families took care of *us*, welcoming my family with such generosity it shocked us and left us unsure how to act or how to be. I recognize their openness now as a central embodiment of the gift culture, a pure counterpoint to the dominant American way of life so tied to transaction and capital. In a quantum world, echoing Walt Whitman's prophetic song and Coretta Scott and Martin Luther King's dream, mercy triumphs over justice perhaps because on a cellular level individuals and cultures contain multitudes. Justice then is renewed on the personal and familial level through authentic moral and cultural authority.

Early on I recall my mother complimenting Cleveland's mother Cecelia about the turquoise bracelet, earrings, and ring she wore, set in rare silver encasements.

"Your jewelry is gorgeous!"

That Christmas, carrying a velvet box in her hands, Cecelia visited my mother.

"Please open it," Cecelia said.

Inside were the earrings, the bracelet, and the ring.

"I can't take these," my mother said.

"I want you to have them," Cecelia said. "From my people to yours."

My mother cried, and often cried again when she thought of the gift from that day forward. They became friends and shared another unifying bond: their husbands' and sons' devotion to basketball. Cheyenne players are among the most decorated of Montana high school basketball legends, always striving to win the elusive state championship. When championship teams form, basketball becomes a powerful expression of the pride of the tribe. Cheyenne teams are known for their speed, uncanny passing, exceptional shooting, and stifling full court defense. In our second year there, my dad as head coach, the team marched all the way to the State tournament. I'll never forget how the families honored their victories. During warm-ups before the first State tournament game, each player and each coach wore a full-length eagle feather headdress donated for the occasion by the family of a chief. The beadwork was intricate and elegant. The front feathers of the headdresses flared back from the face before trailing from the shoulder blades to the floor. The Cheyenne families used sacred regalia to honor those boys as young warriors who had accomplished remarkable things.

When I think of Lafe, Russell, Blake, and Cleveland, I think of life and death. All too often, the basketball heroes of the Cheyenne end up dead or defeated by reservation life. On the reservation it can feel as if bereavement never ceases.

A few years back, when my father and I returned to put on a basketball clinic with Lafe I was reminded of how rare talent sometimes resides in such remote places. It was very good to see Russell and Cleveland again. Blake was an unspoken emptiness and sorrow between us. At the lunch break, Lafe and I played two on two against some of the young high school stars. The passing and shooting were clean as mountain water, the old rhythms with each other easily recalled. When it was over, we spent time laughing and reminiscing, and before I left, Lafe and I pledged to play some independent basketball tournaments together in the future. "We're old," he said. "But still good." There was light in Lafe's smile, and warmth in his eyes.

Lafe leads the Northern Cheyenne Tribal Housing Authority now and coaches the new Cheyenne talents. He wants to help them live well and gain strength in this world. We both seek a certain light for our children and the children of all our loved ones. That light, not unlike the light of dawn or the light of spring, dispels some of the chaos of the American shadow, placing that shadow in grave relief.

Like people, the land receives light and reflects light, or depending on the weather, it doesn't. I'm still struck by the knowledge that much of the forgiveness I've experienced was first given by Lafe, Russell, Blake, and Cleveland in the friendship they offered. Recently I was invited to be a part of a day of forgiveness, helping with unity between Cheyenne, Crow, and white people on the Cheyenne reservation. The Cheyenne and Crow elders, women, and men, asked me to join them in a sacred Mass at the end of the day. The processional cross bore the body of a Cheyenne self-sacrificial warrior in a circle of eagle feathers and the distinctive coats of animals such as badger or bear. Like my father before me, the elders invited me forward to the altar where they wrapped me in a blanket symbolizing love, welcome and well-being. Elizabeth Barrett Browning wrote, "through all hopes that keep us brave, / farther off or nigher, / love me for the house and grave, / and for something higher."

The grit and grace of the wilderness is not unlike our most beloved relationships.

In this light, wilderness and humanity are one.

On Violence and Faith

from an interview live online with The Nervous Breakdown

Brad Listi (BL): Okay. I figure we should get this show on the road. Shann Ray, thanks for joining us today about your story collection, *American Masculine.*

Johnny Evison (JE): I feel like some of the best writers are those who have enjoyed unique experiences growing up. Tell me a little about being one of the only white kids on the rez.

SR: The rez was a fascinating blend of fear and joy. My brother and I and one other guy were the only white kids. Basketball is a form of salvation there. It helped me immensely. Also, humor is like cash, and I love humor, so that was great. I'm returning there two weeks from now to put on a basketball clinic in Lame Deer. My nicknames on the rez are Salt, and Casper the Friendly Ghost. My best friend's nickname is Pepper.

JE: How much of *American Masculine* is autobiographical?

SR: There's only one story that is directly autobiographical, though that one also has a major sidetrack from autobiography.

BL: And which story is that?

SR: That story is "3 from Montana" (which appears here in *The Souls of Others* as "The Family with Their Faces to the Sky"). In reality my bro didn't die. In a way, though, the beatings we receive are symbolic deaths. The rest of the stories have their threads from real life. Many of the white and Native names and people are real, many of the occurrences, the violent ones and the very tender ones, are from moments I've witnessed in family or on the rez or across Montana.

JE: "3 From Montana" is a powerful story. How about father issues? I know it can be tough when your dad is the coach.

SR: There is that large abyss we all must cross in the name of father, I believe, and it is fraught with dangers. Also, the imperiled interior pursues us like a large beast. And there is the hope that a return to the real experience of father, not the false or empty or vacuous or over-hungry, will draw us to a place of deeper reality and thus deeper peace.

JE: Boy, that answer sounds kinda' political! Sort of deftly evasive. Of course, I'm just a nosy S.O.B.

BL: That's good. We like nosey around here. Shann's on the hot seat!

SR: Alright. Put the question right where you want it. The father issues? You mean my own, JE?

JE: I ask because I've got all kinds of father issues. Most of the coach's sons I grew up with had it pretty tough. That is, the competitive coaches.

SR: My dad was an ultra-huge presence. It was like we walked in his shadow and in that shadow there was immense pain and fear and the will to please and the will to hate.

Thankfully, other father figures helped me understand how to embrace his weaknesses, as they exist in me, and do some good long years' work to embody forgiveness, not just of him, but also involving my own asking forgiveness for the ways I'd silenced him and over-condemned him. Father issues are like blood in America. Everyone alive has some.

BL: So, you're a professor of leadership and forgiveness studies at Gonzaga. How do you teach someone to lead? How do you teach someone to forgive?

JE: Forgiveness is powerful stuff.

SR: A deep question, leadership and forgiveness. In forgiveness, I think of my mother forgiving my dad, and my dad forgiving his father and mother, and that mystery is enough to take me all the way to the far shore, even if the boat is sometimes small and beset with oceanic chasms and waves like mountains.

In leadership, I value Greenleaf's notion that true leadership evokes in self and others greater wisdom, health, freedom, and autonomy, and it serves the least privileged of society or at least does not do greater harm.

Greenleaf was an iconoclast. A vice president at AT&T when they had 1 million employees. A Quaker. A reader. A thinker. A person of heart married to a person of perhaps deeper heart (he would say). He was a contemporary of Robert Frost, E.B. White, and Rabbi Heschel, and knew them. He also wrote a gorgeous essay on Frost's poem "Directive." He was kind of a philosopher poet who also happened to lead one of the world's largest corporations through the 1940s, 50s, and 60s, living like a modern prophet, changing the face of the American corporation through diverse hires, speaking revolutionary ideas like "All white people should get out of positions of leadership," and retiring early to affirm that revolution, to teach and write and live simply in Quaker community.

LLZ: Do you believe leadership capabilities are innate or can fully be taught?

JE: Great question, LLZ.

SR: I believe leadership can be taught, however, the place each person starts (with personality, temperament, personal gifts, collective gifts, psychological understanding, depth of balance between love and power) are very different. So for some, the ability to lead in a way that draws humanity to a more transparent experience of the world is very far away, demands years of mentoring and may be unattainable, while for others, the pathway is more natural if gradual, humbling, and equally demanding. Greenleaf called these people the true natural servants of society, who serve the highest priority needs of others. He saw it as one to one, or in the context of a small group of mutually caring individuals he called *primus inter pares*, or "first among equals," meaning if the honor of leadership is present then that leadership must be shared, and communal. To him, leadership is worthy only if the leader's (or leaders') heart(s) align with serving the highest priority needs of others. Of course, the imbalance and narcissistic drive is never far from any of us. On one side, those with excessive ego resulting in power hunger. On the other, the co-dependent or those afraid of power. Both are forms of narcissism or over-abundant self-focus.

EOL: Can you talk a bit about your writing process? I realize this is a bit of a common question, but I'm always curious how different writers approach their work. For example: do you work everyday? How long did it take you to write the stories in *American Masculine*?

SR: Thanks, EOL. The stories in *American Masculine* were written over a12-year span. Outside of the fallow times, I tend to consistently try to work on various things (poems, short stories, essays, social science, novels, etc.). Having three daughters, I'm often at ballet lessons and the like, so I normally work on stories and poems there. I try to keep 10pm-1am the hours for writing and reading and being quiet and listening. If I go past 1am, which I do when a fire sets in, I get ugly to live with.

BL: Heh. Talk to Evison.

JE: I'm so hard to live with, my wife makes me go camping by myself.

SR: And to get back to your comment on politics, JE, it would be kind of fun to get a cadre of writers together to assault the bastions of political power with some supple and torqued philosophies of individual and collective life together. We ready?

BL: Vaçlav Havel.

SR: I love Havel. Consciousness precedes Being; his evocative poetics of the Velvet Revolution. I'm of Czech heritage myself.

BL: How close are you to your roots there? Do you feel a strong ethnic tie?

JE: I sense that you certainly feel a pull toward your background in Montana–that is, living all those years on the rez.

SR: I feel close to my Czech roots. Much of my research in forgiveness as the counterweight to violence in the world has come from the Czech lands, the Velvet Revolution, the tragedy and triumph of Lidice, a town where the Nazis massacred so many, and where years later, reconciliation came. I'm of German heritage too, which in the context of Lidice is excruciating. Humbling. Czech authors offer a central heritage to me. Klima and Kundera and many others.

JE: Hrabal!

SR: Yes, Hrabal! The fate of tumbling from that window at 82 while feeding the birds, or was flying to his death a choice? How life understands us.

In light of the reservation the sense of family, warmth, and all-encompassing love I've received from Cheyenne, Crow, Blackfeet, and Lakota families is not something I can replace.

BL: All of this Havel talk actually brings up an interesting question, vis-à-vis leadership. As someone who studies leadership for a living, what are your views on political leadership? Things are so ugly in the world, and in Washington D.C. here at home. I sometimes wonder if it's even possible for someone to effectively lead at that level. You look at a guy like Havel, who couldn't be a better example of the principled revolutionary, and even he seemed to struggle when power actually became his. Am I too cynical? (I hate to throw you such a broad, bottomless question…it just seems like politics is where good leaders go to die.)

SR: You bring up a great point, Brad. The fact that evil and good co-exist and are perhaps in an embrace —

something like life, or death, or sex, or dance. I do believe the world is sometimes too cynical, which leads to greater nihilism, which leads to objectification of humanity and despair… but then again that likely leads to the sledge and rot and thick brown earth from which new life comes: a systems philosophy, and also one that many artists I know tend to identify with in order to take them below the veneer of cynicism.

BL: Figuratively, usually. Literally, sometimes.

SR: I do know a number of politicians whose interior life is gorgeous. And then again, there's Weiner.

BL: Man. Weiner. You can't write this stuff.

SR: My wife and I, both being trained in psychology, laughed for an hour when we found out his name is Weiner. Get your name legally changed before the bad press hits.

BL: So here's one more question related to your profession — what is a "systems psychologist?"

(Your *other* profession, I should say.)

SR: Systems psychology is akin to systems in biology and the science behind the biological notion of feedback loops and homeostasis, static and dynamic elements that are hard to discern, though definitely comprehensible. When authentic insight or depth of awareness is gained in a family system, or organizational system, or national system, small movements can create tremendous change. Though it always takes time, of course. For example, research shows it takes three to five years for character change in a person from the point of total brokenness or total willingness to change.

Gloria: Hello!! Is the party still happening? Did the keg blow?

BL: We're still here, Gloria. Welcome! Look out!

Gloria: Listi throws down the gauntlet and assumes I'm afraid.

SR: Couldn't help it. He had to get some basketball trash in there.

Gloria: It's what he calls his mom.

SR: Thank you for that vintage body blow you just gave JE, Gloria!

JE: I've got a couple mom zingers I could come back with, but I better not.

BL: We're already devolving at a pretty nice clip here. Part of our rich tradition.

Gloria: What is it about ranch life in Montana?

SR: There is that good scent of horsehair, after the horse has broken a sweat. A favorite of mine. My grandpa had a huge Palomino horse. I'd lay on that horse's back as a boy and smell the coat and fall asleep.

JE: If American Masculine were a cologne what would it smell like?

Gloria: No, if *American Masculine* were a car, what kind of car would it be?

SR: Definitely a number of great cars come to mind. The huge Cadillacs of the 70s, Chevy trucks of the 50s, 60s, and 70s. How about for you all?

BL: I'm thinking a Hummer. Though that might be overly compensatory. Jeep?

SR: My wife saw my dad's Corvette once, sitting like a gem in the garage. She said, and I quote: "Does this make you feel like a bigger man?" He sold it a year later.

BL: What year was the 'Vette?

SR: The 'Vette was a 90 I believe. He'd had it for a few years, very nice, silver. But I think he felt like it was too much, drew too much attention. He's a truck guy and an old cheap car guy. We had 5 or 6 vehicles for $100 or less growing up. Rust holes in the floorboards. See the road beneath your feet at 70 miles an hour.

BL: Rumor has it that your mother grew up in the town of Cohagen, Montana. Population: 8. And it had a store and two bars! True story?

SR: True story. Great town, out in the wide open eastern plains of Montana. I spent summers there with my bro. Small ranch with some cattle. Horse or two.

BL: Sounds idyllic.

Gloria: Idyllic and maybe the perfect place to commit a heinous crime and get away with it…

SR: Not idyllic. Like many Montana youth, I felt bored near to death at times but then there was also the fun of hunting for frogs and snakes and running like a wild animal wherever you wanted to roam.

And yes, the quiet and sometimes not so quiet violence that accompanies a lonely landscape.

BL: In a recent interview you did with *The Barking*, you said the following and it really struck me:

"After my mother and father had some tumultuous years, the family came to believe in each other more fully and experienced some much-needed healing by seeking a congruent family life in the context of belief in a power beyond ourselves. I was about 10 years old and from that point, when formerly my family was largely agnostic or at least functionally atheist, we began to listen and seek to understand in an entirely new way. The changes were long in coming, but uncommon, refreshing, and restored us to each other. In our case I'm convinced we would have completely fractured, individually and collectively, without those changes. The Christian tradition, though I realize it has been very painful for some, became a true power to us over the years and in fact made us more grateful for each other, and better able to live for each other."

BL: Can you talk about this a bit more? I'm curious how this conversion happened. Was there someone who guided it or did you just start going to church?

SR: Great question. My mother's close friend, Lori, is one of those people in whose presence you feel physically near to the center of life, or near to God, or very near to what I experience as love. She built a devoted and fluid friendship with my mom and that's what started it. Lori's life personified a faith that had emotional, intellectual, and soulful depth and met our lives like a train at the station. My mom and brother and I jumped on, gladly. A year later, my father did too, through his own pain in fracturing the family and his desire to return to something he felt he'd lost. They did good hard work rebuilding and forgiving, and then working to change their lives in order to be less hard on each other. In the church we went to we encountered many people with easy kindness. I think they knew something of Greenleaf's *primus inter pares* and it came forth like song and enveloped our family. That church was not without its faults of course, but such faults of human hypocrisy exist everywhere, in the person of faith as well as the agnostic or the atheist, and regardless of faith or nonfaith in my experience real results with regard to family, community, and national health or wholeness come from people living with integrity, one by one and together, living from a sense of wholeness in a balance of love and power.

BL: Wow. Well, that sounds like a really compelling Christian experience. (As compared to, say, my Catholic experience.)

Gloria: I didn't enjoy Christianity, ever.

SR: I think for me, not having had church experiences and really having a home experience that was laced with alcohol and hard living and some violence and a lot of infidelity, when that started to change, the desire that exists (I believe in all people) to live in order to love well was like topping those vistas in the Beartooth range in southern Montana and seeing the world again as if for the first time.

Gloria: I will say the way you describe Lori… people like her always made me appreciate those who live their faith in an honorable way.

SR: Living life in an honorable way is a beautiful thing.

BL: I suppose it depends on how it's taught — and by whom. And in what context, and so on.

SR: I agree. But of course the abuses of thought and emotion and spirit tend to undercut it all—be the abuser religious, spiritual, anti-religious, or atheist. I find that to be true everywhere.

BL: Thanks, Shann, and before we let you go we're going to subject you to our vaunted "Lightning Round."

SR: Yes!

BL: The way the Lightning Round works: We ask you a series of rapid-fire "either/or" questions and you respond in a word or two, quickly.

SR: Got it.

BL: Salinger or Carver?

SR: Carver.

BL: Beer or whiskey?

SR: Whiskey for sure.

BL: Emerson or Thoreau?

SR: Emerson.

BL: Magic or Bird?

SR: Isaiah Thomas.

BL: Heh.

SR: But not as a GM or a coach.

BL: (No kidding!)

BL: Pessimistic optimist or optimistic pessimist?

SR: Healthy skepticism.

Gloria: Kirk or Picard?

SR: Picard in a minute.

BL: Mozart or Beethoven?

SR: "Ode to Joy" is impossible to beat.

Gloria: Facebook or Twitter.

SR: Facebook. I like pictures.

BL: Binge writer or disciplined writer?

SR: In dry times neither. In writing times both.

BL: Bacon or steak?

SR: Steak with bacon on top, and gravy.

Gloria: Binge or purge?

SR: Binge all the way.

BL: "Kill your television" or "Love my TiVo!"?

SR: I love to murder televisions.

BL: In the wilds of Montana.

SR: Walking outside any day, over the tube sucking me in.

BL: Alright, Gloria. Hit him with one more.

Gloria: Ebook or book in print?

SR: The physical specimen in my hands, the pages, the shadow, the light.

Gloria: Perfect.

Gloria: Family conflict – drama – makes a good book.

Eros and Logos:

Leadership, Poetry, Feminism, and the Critical Unities of Gender Well-being

The feminist warrior poet Audre Lorde died in St. Croix in 1992. She lived as a freedom fighter seeking to serve the deepest needs of people in order to create a more just world. Her critique of dominant patriarchy resounds: "The master's tools will never dismantle the master's house. They may allow us to temporarily beat him at his own game, but they will never enable us to bring about genuine change." In the truest sense of the word, Lorde led people and nations into greater love and freedom. With her life and poetry she showed how the legitimate power associated with serving the highest priority needs of others can help heal the heart of the peoples of the world, especially the least respected or those Cornel West identifies as the wretched of the earth, a moniker imbued with clarion transparency by Frantz Fanon: the least of these being those we are unified with, indebted to, and with whom we share humility, *humus*, the earth that bears the imprint of our feet and the hope of a more humane existence. Ill patriarchal tendencies wound the world, leaving in their wake power abuses of all forms, severe lack of emotional intelligence, hyper-rational lack of love, a history of genocide, and the aftereffects of the generational narcissistic injury so prevalent in America today. Lorde, a self-described "black, lesbian, mother, warrior, womanist, poet" who lived and created through directly challenging intersectional injustice wrote in *The Black Unicorn*:

and when we speak we are afraid
our words will not be heard
nor welcomed
but when we are silent
we are still afraid
So it is better to speak
remembering
we were never meant to survive

Her boldness helps us overcome our fears, and draws me to a question asked of me by the inimitable Nike Imoru, a North Londoner raised in Nigeria, an exceptional casting director, and the first woman and person of color to gain a tenured position in the Theatre Department at Hull in the UK when she was only twenty-eight. Like Audre, Nike's presence is water from a deep well.

The question: What is your understanding of the masculine in America?

Lest we, like the structurally racist system in which we are embedded, become too binary or too set on defining gender it's good to be reminded the amount of feminine or masculine in each person chromosomally is a mystery, a uniquely conceived blend in every individual. We house within us the non-binary dualism or rather multivalent multiplicity of a feminine/masculine artistic and biological notion, a circularity of which no one can claim full knowledge. Art sings and science confirms humanity's inability to control, contain, or fully name ultimate truth. With that humility in mind, in light of unrelenting systemic patriarchal power imbalances, an extreme mediocrity exists in much of the masculine in America today, characterized by emptiness, impoverished relational capacity, an overblown or under-developed sense of self, and a life with others that is often devoid of meaning. Such men are filled of things like excess media, sexual objectification, emotional shallowness, and the man's agenda at the expense of others, the age-old establishment of overt and covert patriarchal footing. No words for feelings. Violence. Privilege for privilege sake, which results in decadence, and in the end decay, and finally death. The Western world is currently experiencing this decadence, decay, and death. Carl Jung gave a lucid and fear-invoking expression of the masculine and the feminine. In Jung's conception the masculine is symbolized as the logos, which he referred to as the power to make meaning, to be meaningful, and to be experienced as meaningful by loved ones and by the collective soul around us. Not the super-rational man, incapable of emotion or regret, but the person who lives well, loves well, and is well loved. A question then rises, how many men do you know who are experienced as meaningful in their relationships with women and men, with their children, with others?

A modern practitioner of a form of leadership called servant-leadership, Robert K. Greenleaf, embodied lesser-known aspects of holistic living such as prophesy, foresight, healing, and the will to better society, often through personal and collective sacrifice. Not servant as slave or as subservient, but servant to the highest priority needs of others, a concept referred to by black thought leader Lea E. Williams as reserved for those we consider *servants of the people*. Through this subtle embodiment in both life and poetry, let alone the ambiguous term leadership, a subtle authentic force is exerted: the dynamic, steadying, and fiercely graceful impulse toward repentance, atonement, and forgiveness at the core of humanity. Greenleaf died in 1990, just two years before Audre Lorde. The true test of our humanity and whether we truly serve, love, and lead, according to Greenleaf, is that others around us become more wise, more free, more autonomous, more healthy, and better able to serve others; and the least privileged of society are benefited, or at least not further deprived. I often think Greenleaf is describing not just leaders across the disciplines, but especially the transgressive poets through whom we've encountered a more generous sense of life.

Greenleaf's test, difficult to administer, and worthy of humanity's most hard-won humility, utterly lays low the white supremacist patriarchal regime bell hooks so eloquently detailed in *Feminist Theory: From Margin to Center*. In hooks' understanding, aligned with Greenleaf's best test of human nature, we are authentically whole if we are simultaneously broken. In a form of existential vitality and surrender, awareness, foresight, and healing accompany us. This way of living or leading, as a person, as a poet, removes power from our hands and acknowledges legitimate moral and relational gravity resides in the hands of the beloved other. I can't bend my family members' or friends' arms behind their backs and force them to tell others I've become less toxic or more loving, more whole. I've either done the life work required and their voice resounds freely or I need to seek more healing. In equal measure this is true not just of individuals but of nation states and all privileged or toxically dominant cultures. Groups small or large who listen and respond to beloved others' subtle and direct demands for atonement through reparations enter the restorative essence to which life inherently calls the human community.

In his telling essay on Robert Frost's poem "Directive," Greenleaf sought to affirm the nonlinear, mystery-based, and circular wisdom more readily associated with poets and painters than with business practitioners or social scientists, and in so doing, he called leaders across the disciplines to take more responsibility for their own humanity and for humanity as a whole. Often in both ancient literature and contemporary social science the linear or rational is more associated with the traditional masculine while circular or mystery-based ways of knowing are projected as more associated with the traditional feminine. To be a leader responsible for the healing so vitally important to the wholeness of individuals and society, the mystery of gender wholeness along the she, he, they continuum, and the reality of repair, forgiveness, and making things right or whole again comes forth from the shadows, illuminating often obscured and gritty truths.

Greenleaf's essay "The Inward Journey" relates how his reading Frost's "Directive" deepened his understanding of the courageous and wise presence of the servant as leader. Though the extent of Greenleaf's personal connection with Robert Frost is unknown, they did know each other, and spent time in each other's presence. The possibility that they directly influenced one another's thought is apparent. Consider this moment, relayed by Greenleaf:

> In a group conversation with him [Frost] one evening, he digressed on the subject of loyalty. At one point I interjected with: "Robert, that is not the way you have defined loyalty before."
>
> He turned to me with a broad friendly grin and asked softly, "How did I define it?"
>
> I replied, "In your talk on Emerson a few years ago, you said, 'Loyalty is that for the lack of which your gang will shoot you without benefit of trial by jury.'"
>
> To this man who had struggled without recognition until he was forty, and then had to move to England to get it, nothing could have pleased him more in his old age than to have an obscure passage like this quoted to him in a shared give-and-take with non-literary people.

In Greenleaf's engagement with Frost's poem, he affirmed the necessity of a prophetic, circular orientation in going further into the depths of human awareness: "Our problem is circular: we must understand in order to be able to understand. It has something to do with awareness and symbols." Symbolic understanding is formless, cannot be linearized, and cannot be understood by simple 1-2-3 progressions. Rather, it is absorbed; it is an element of life in which the poet, the transgressive and revolutionary quiet or more overt leader, chooses to become willingly submerged. Greenleaf continued:

Awareness, letting something significant and disturbing develop between oneself and a symbol, comes more by being waited upon rather than by being asked. One of the most baffling of life's experiences is to stand beside one who is aware, one who is looking at a symbol and is deeply moved by it, and, confronting the same symbol, to be unmoved. Oh, that we could just be open in the presence of symbols that cry out to speak to us, let our guards down, and take the risks of being moved!

The power of a symbol is measured by its capacity to sustain a flow of significant new meaning. The substance of the symbol may be a painting, a poem or story, allegory, myth, scripture, a piece of music, a person, a crack in the sidewalk, or a blade of grass. Whatever or whoever, it produces a confrontation in which much that makes the symbol meaningful comes from the beholder.

The potentiality is both in the symbol and in the beholder.

We might say poets and more overt societal leaders share the same interior faults. By extension, the leader or poet with a leader-first or ambition-first mentality, often mired in self-aggrandizement without foreknowledge, ambition at the expense of love and service, and an inappropriate power drive obscuring or negating authentic intimacy, generally lacks healthy self-awareness. The leader-first ambition-first leader or poet has limited or no capacity to name his or her own faults, let alone invite others to influence, challenge, or help correct them. In this light,

Greenleaf's prophetic truths—warning individuals, communities, and nations against the leader-first mentality—take on pivotal, essential meaning.

Reynolds's qualitative social science study through a feminist lens used content analysis methodology to better understand speeches delivered by fifty of the top female and male American business leaders whose companies made *Fortune* best-of lists. Kae Reynolds holds a PhD in leadership studies, and has taught in 7 different countries, including Saudi Arabia where she was one of few foreign women invited to teach leadership. She is a graceful and powerful leader who fluently speaks 5 languages. Reynolds took a precise deep dive into whether gender differences among prominent American business leaders support the conceptualization that servant-leadership is a gender-integrative mode of leadership and found servant-leadership gender integration intuitively and phenomenologically resonant. In her study important gender differences were observed: for example, women spoke more about humility and standing back in leadership, whereas men highlighted accountability; and female speakers considered the motivation to lead as an ethical drive and a choice, whereas male speakers articulated it as an obligation.

In Reynold's study, gender differences found in her analysis could reify traditional gender congruency expectations if read without critical gender understanding. To counteract such reification, her study presented evidence of female leaders combining care orientation and relationality (typically feminine aspects of "leadership" in social science) with courage and contrarian thinking (typically masculine aspects of "leadership" in social science) and evidence of male leaders combining accountability and risk taking (typically masculine aspects) with forgiveness and being attuned to others' needs (typically feminine aspects). Reynolds concluded that servant-leadership combines both feminine and masculine aspects of leadership.

Greenleaf's interpretations of the etymology of "servant" and "leader" return the words to their original and imperative communal meanings—serving and leading others through healthy self-sacrifice, by sacrificing ego, power, and ambition for the good of the community, especially the community's children, elders, and most marginalized peoples. Greenleaf spoke to the value of the words *servant* and *leader* symbolically, across gender, culture, time, and context. Reynolds argued that the combination of servant facets and leader facets of servant-leadership does not automatically confirm the negatives that can be associated with gendered notions of "servant" and "leader" but, on the contrary, provides a model of ethical and gender equity-enhancing leadership. Poets, in our quietness or in the trumpet call of a transcendent feeling, also lead society and therefore knowledge of leadership may prove necessary to enhance a poet's understanding. According to Reynolds, servant-leadership can serve as "a driving force for generating discourse on gender-integrative approaches" to life and leadership. Reynolds proposed that the paradoxical linguistic term *servant-leader* is not a disguise for male-centric norms, as scholars such as Eicher-Catt have claimed, but a complementary and harmonious dualism. Jiying Song, scholar of leadership studies, wrote:

This dualism resonates with the concepts of *yin* and *yang*, which represent female and male, respectively, in ancient Chinese literature.

As for yin and yang, they are the Way of heaven and earth, the fundamental principles [governing] the myriad beings, father and mother to all changes and transformations, the basis and beginning of generating life and killing, the palace of spirit brilliance.

Lao Tzu said, "All the myriad things carry the Yin on their backs and hold the Yang in their embrace, deriving their vital harmony from the proper blending of the two vital Breaths." *Yin* and *yang* cannot exist without each other. They are a contradictory yet complementary unit. Women were degraded in ancient China based on the ascendancy of patriarchy, the focus on the contradictory aspect of *yin* and *yang*, and the elevation of *yang*. The same kind of degradation still exists in the leadership field today. Having stressed the equally and mutually complementary character of *yin-yang*, some scholars paved the way for the women's egalitarian movement in nineteenth-century China. Likewise, this is what Reynolds and many other servant-leadership scholars are doing—elevating complementary aspects of gender without neglecting the contradictory aspects. Carrying yin and holding yang in intimate embrace, leaders learn to forgive more readily and more deeply, and help others gain the vital harmony so often missing in today's families, organizations, and nations.

Through a discussion of the complementary character of *yin-yang* and servant-leader elements, without ignoring the contradictory aspects, leaders may establish harmony and gender-integrative models wherever they serve. Although the results of Reynolds's study indicated that gender stereotyping continues to affect conceptualizations of leadership, her study also provided evidence of servant-leaders crossing gender boundaries and integrating gendered traits and behaviors. As Reynolds noted, by integrating the female perspective with a male perspective, a paradigm shift in leadership theory (through avenues inherent to servant-leadership) has the capacity to move organizations from hierarchy-driven, rules-based, and authoritative models to value-driven, follower-oriented, and participative models with gender balance.

This brings me to the good involved in multiple views, and to the Jesuit and Quaker notions, often identifiably feminist, of the need for persuasion rather than coercion, listening rather than over-talking, and the timeless truth that among many good possibilities the mature person seeks ultimate good with and for others. We affirm Jung's typology as well as the current complexities that exist in human relations by noticing that each of us have both feminine and masculine within us and the extent to which we hide or subdue either of these, we harm ourselves and others.

Jung conceived of the feminine as the eros, but not the blown-out glammed and glitzed porn culture of American media and Westernized masculine agendas. Neither is it the critical, enraged, contempt-focused feminine at odds with the masculine. Rather, he conceptualized the eros as the womblike existence that gives peace, the life-giving sacrificial essence willing to undergo great suffering in order to preserve more authentic life, the wild mystery at odds with all who might try to come against the child, the family, the collective, or the future. For me, Mochis comes to mind, the Cheyenne woman warrior whose ferocity is legendary. After the Sand Creek Massacre in the late 1800s in which US Cavalry slaughtered the Cheyenne, Mochis took up the axe and fought as a warrior and killed many for eleven years until she was captured and shipped by train to Florida where she was incarcerated by the United States Army as a Prisoner of War. My mother comes to mind, with her bravery and her heart of forgiveness, and my wife with her radiance, power, and wisdom. Not to mention my Czech grandmother. In our family, we call her the Great One. Each of these, in their own way, reflect bell hooks' liberatory ethic founded in critical race theory and Angela Davis' and Judith Butler's restorative wisdom founded in critical feminism aimed at overthrowing prejudicial supremacist patriarchal regimes. What rises from this overthrow, through revolutionary love and leadership, is a communal existence closer to dialogue than monologue, closer to care than apathy or alienation, and closer to peace than war.

It is increasingly clearer how often the masculine seeks to subdue and overtake the feminine. The masculine is infatuated with a pseudo-eros, an eros he himself has pumped up to proportions that amount to oblivion. The resulting rape-culture that rises from such malevolent masculinity cannot face its own feminine, for to do so would shatter the man who bears it. He would then have to willingly face further ego-fracture, seeking to integrate the feminine, honor the feminine and truly love the feminine in order to be healed and made whole. In like fashion the feminine has often estranged and alienated the masculine, setting itself against the masculine through bitter disaffection or outright hatred, a form of condemnation that amounts to giving the masculine pariah status, often naming the masculine as meaningless or absurd not only in the core of relationships, but also at national and international levels. That form of feminine cannot face its own masculine, for to do so would be too shattering and would then require the feminine to integrate the masculine, to take him in with care and enduring affection as well as legitimate healing-oriented power, to truly love in order to be healed and made whole. In my experience working with women, men, and gender-diverse people as a systems psychologist, we carry mutual desolation in our hands. We are made of bone and blood, heart, and spirit. Understanding and love are required if we are to embrace and heal the feminine and the masculine inside ourselves and in our relationships with others.

Modern day prophets such as Lorde, hooks, Davis, and Butler see far into the mystery, depicting men who are often dis-integrated, void, violent, cold, apathetic, at odds with the feminine and in effect, at odds with themselves. Some of these men, including many I know, desire to move and change and become capable of giving and receiving love. In symbiotic conflict with the harsh masculine, Lorde, hooks, Davis, and Butler also note many women live silenced or enraged, embittered, hateful and integrally ill at ease with the masculine. Some of these women also desire an unfolding that results in unity over fragmentation. But across the sanctity of the gender spectrum to become humble requires being humbled. I know such people personally, whose shadows extend and do harm, who are sometimes blessed to come into what bell hooks calls "redemptive love," and who have wept at the beauty that exists when they let themselves be broken and let themselves emerge from a long agonizing darkness into something new.

There is an essence to life, to lived experience, in which we kiss the earth, in effect eating our own humiliation. In my own life the will to surrender or submit to the redemptive love hooks refers too has often been elusive, and pride too present. I am reminded of how silent and songlike, how contemplative and prayerful the writing life is. "You must grasp life in its depths," van Gogh said. In response, the poet crafts poems, the novelist novels, the short story writer stories, that show love and respect for the grand, ominous landscapes of humanity and the world. The result is rigorous honesty with regard to the shadow and light in people, in families of all forms, profoundly diverse in the interior life and the life of the collective. There has long been a philosophy that says the landscape, and the human tumult, grind you up and spit you out, so watch out or your head might get taken off. The mountains kill you. The animals kill you. Your family and friends kill you. Life kills you. Yet in reading hooks and Lorde, this feels too absolute, too darkly nihilistic. In them I'm reminded the artist who serves humanity serves life.

I'm reminded the artist who serves life, serves love.

In the wake of authentic love comes a deeply felt sense of dignity. Internationally, I find this dignity often attends a holistic conception of the Divine. Cornel West spoke of

W.E.B. Du Bois's (*The Souls of Black Folk*, *The Talented Tenth*, etc.) spirituality saying Du Bois was "more of a prophet than most Christians or religious Jews or religious Buddhists and so on, because… he was able to sustain himself spiritually without the apparatus of tradition." West noted with hardy respect how Du Boise didn't succumb to the reductionistic (and in fact, masculinist) bias of scientific positivism and the kind of narrow Darwinism plagued by "the more sophomoric atheists like… Christopher Hitchens, Richard Dawkins, and others who reduce the rich Darwin to narrow scientism. Darwin is the brook of fire through which we all must pass." West's uniquely revolutionary Christianity, underlined by his vision of healthy anti-imperialist Marxism, given in everyday life through loving acts of service and the willingness to die for the wretched of the earth, calls on Western powers, especially America, to overthrow the militarism, materialism, racism and poverty imperialism produces, nightshades which have always bred greater patriarchy, sexism, classism, homophobia, and xenophobia. Poisons. In West's sisterhood with bell hooks, I find a genuine sense of heartfelt welcome, identification with the love, justice, and truth embodied by their conception of Christ in the real world, and transmitted by the soul of Christ in historical and present-day Christianity. This Christianity fights for the freedom of others through truth, justice, and love, including the will to die for friends and strangers, and in the words of Nazim Hikmet, Marxist and transcendent Islamic poet, the willingness to die even for those you know nothing of. This Christ, of which Cornel West, James Cone (*The Cross and the Lynching Tree*) and bell hooks speak, is not bound by undue optimism or facile understandings of grace, but sees clearly into the murky oblivion at the core of humanity, the Beckett-drawn existential emptiness of our collective evil, and stands courageously against it even to the point of death. Being a believer in Christ, like West I find it "true that my atheistic brothers and sisters do not accept conceptions of God linked to love and justice as I do. But atheistic movement can be one of the carriers of prophetic tradition." A community mosaic colored by love, truth, justice, beauty, and goodness, the transcendentals of which the Jesuits (or "little Christs") speak across time, space, and belief (or anti-belief, being another kind of conviction), religious or otherwise, is a community of loving devotion. Of course, like all systems, be it the multiverse of faith traditions worldwide, the uncounted systems in our individual and collective family lives, or the systems of work, government, and public life through which we encounter the world, when rigid, inflexible, and calcified, or when boundaryless, enmeshed, or entangled, trouble and suffering are the result.

Yes, we are harmed. Yes, we die. Together we know these truths. Yet death can be met with love, and trauma with dignity: this we often overlook. Just as life can be embraced with healthy abandon, and togetherness with wisdom. Having grown up in Montana, I've been embedded in the wilderness, the mountains, rivers, and skies of that country, showing me there exists not merely the reality of my vain or vapor-like existence, but also the reality of an enduring sense of generosity, perhaps eternal, and with it, an abiding intimacy, despite and even within the presence of evil, decadence, decay, and death. In bell hooks and Audre Lorde I've found prose and poetry that does not ignore or forego or turn a blind eye to the presence of human evil, but rather, reaches for light in the presence of evil.

To find light in the presence of evil involves foresight.

In great literature, I believe foresight is ever present.

In troubled literary art, just as in unhealthy individuals and families, foresight is often lacking or nonexistent. In healthy art, as in healthy people, the wilderness of the human heart can beckon us toward love. I think of foresight differently as a psychologist than I would if I were trained in another field. When a psychologist lacks foresight the costs are high. People may descend into suicide, or ramp toward homicide. Outside of troubling mental health deficits, even in "normal" people a lack of foresight is a symbol of relational disorder. Though painful to face, when we lack foresight, life holds us responsible. For dominant culture, consequence is a difficult concept, specifically in present day America where it is so easy to be irresponsible across the dominant/non-dominant divide: in the family or at work, and on a larger scale in the way America engages with the marginalized and with other countries. Being that America, like all nations, contains manifold complexities, when America lacks foresight collectively the results are ruinous. In poetry, as in the discernment involved in leading nations, there is a need to hone our capacity for foresight. So when I think about it from a psychological perspective, I think, how can we train ourselves toward more foresight? And when I think of art, I ask how can we hone foresight in our artistic leanings?

Examples from the Gottman Institute's research on relationships provide unique clarity. Research conducted there shows a level of foresight never before realized in social science. In three to five minutes a Gottman-trained therapist can predict at a 95% rate how likely a couple is to fracture or descend further into "negative sentiment override," a level of negative feeling and experience in which the relationship is plagued by impending dissolution rather than essential unification. The institute's founder, John Gottman, and his wife Julie, also discovered that 80% of men who divorce all share one character quality, while 80% of women who divorce share a different but mutually reinforcing character quality.

So what are these detrimental qualities?

According to the Gottmans' research, 80% of men who divorce refuse to receive the influence of the feminine, and 80% of women who divorce have contempt for the masculine.

Such an imploding dynamic in human relations then becomes distilled as foresight when it's turned toward health: women who relate well affirm and love the masculine; and men who relate well receive the influence of the feminine and love the feminine. The whole person who relates well listens to and loves both the feminine and the masculine. In light of this, some suffering, generationally-bound, is unavoidable, while other suffering when met with foresight becomes predictable and can be turned away from. The Gottman Institute research is tied to a systemic way of looking at the world, and has proven to be of equal significance across age, gender, and sexual orientation: if I am this type of person I'm generally going to attract that type of person. If I don't receive the influence of others, I attract contempt and evoke relational dissolution. If I am full of contempt, I attract people who are defensive, who put up a wall in their interactions with me, and who often refuse to receive my influence. Again, I evoke dissolution. The same principles are reflected not only in organizational life, national policy, and global interactions, but also in poetry, short stories, novels, and creative nonfiction. Often, artistic fields seem to be excluded from in-depth psychological analysis, but the same underlying discernments exist in the heart of art as in the heart of humanity. If I'm cynical I tend to attract opposition. If I'm depressed or unduly angry, anxious, or difficult to relate to, I tend to attract an equal but opposing desultory force. Similarly, the person who is humble or graced with common sense and self-responsibility, tends to attract healthiness in others. In other words, we attract to ourselves the same level of maturity we have attained. In psychological understanding, this is the disturbing fundamental foresight that you join with or marry an equal level of dysfunction as yourself.

In like fashion, art that embodies shallow understandings of despair, showing contempt for light, generates more despair in the world. Art that embodies the saccharine, obfuscating hard won truths regarding human evil, also generates more despair. Such art, despairing without recourse or spouting platitudes without the recognition of just how darkness inheres, lacks foresight not because it speaks too much death but because it silences, effaces, or erases life. In this sense, great literature counters the homicidal and suicidal tendencies of humanity, with deeper humanity. Be it through comedy or tragedy, through descent or transcendence or both, great art endures because it is fully human without reducing life's integral mystery.

Many of the more curative psychological truths fall under the wing of foresight. We all understand some of these, such as: the only person in the world you can change is yourself. But there are also unwritten truths not as readily discovered that prove helpful not just in life but in discerning the processes involved in creativity. For example, a primary finding of systems psychology states: when you change yourself, others around you have to change. An interesting axiom, and a potent one. So, for example, if in my relationships with others I get more defensive or more fortified or more rigid or more severe in the coming months, it's generally predictable how people will respond to me: they will probably say something like, "What's going on?"; "I don't like this very much."; or "I wish you weren't so difficult to be with." The outlay is also generally predictable. I'm going to make people irritated and, eventually, different types of responses beyond irritation will come my way, like anger, frustration, and attacks on my character. Certain results follow when I become less mature, less fully human.

I believe much of current literary art, by cascading into or becoming overfocused on less responsible expressions, contains less moral gravitas, and therefore less humanity. In other words, as a person and as an artist, I can't give what I don't have. If I don't have much love in my heart, I don't have much love to give, and my art will lack the depths associated with love. If I have too much cynicism, or facile boundarylessness, or a lack of wisdom, my art will not have the magnitude intrinsic to the most enduring understandings of human complexity. In contemporary literature, where facile tragedy is the overlord of meaningful comedy, or facile comedy is the overlord of sacred tragedy, readers experience a poverty of love. In art made whole, love rises through tragedy and comedy, attends to the voicelessness and desperation of which comedy and tragedy speak, and still sings.

On the other hand, if a person changes in order to become more whole, the result is not generally what we think. It doesn't mean life suddenly tips over into healthy relationships. Why? Because all change must be tested. Our biology tests change and requires homeostasis, challenging whether we are really going to change or not. Changing to a fuller way of life or more fully developed moral character will receive resistance from the self and from others, because integrity requires endurance. Integrity is the difference between what systems psychologists call first-order and second-order change. In first-order change, the system changes for a bit and then pops back to the same shape it was in before, maintaining its original homeostasis; in second-order change, the system changes for the long-term, others affirm the change, and the change eventually becomes aligned toward relational health as the system accomplishes a new more holistic homeostasis.

Greenleaf had a wonderful grasp of foresight and the robust futures associated with foresight. He believed not only are people responsible to have foresight, they are individually responsible to create collective responsibility for foresight so that families, communities, and nations can experience greater health, wisdom, freedom, and autonomy, and the least privileged will be benefitted or at least not further deprived. In a larger sense the question is daunting: Will we gather the foresight we need to meaningfully address the current state of the globe, the volatile ways we relate to each other, our apathy and our lack of individual and collective well-being?

In art, as in life, our lives depend on the answer.

How did the Gottman Institute come to understand foresight? How did social science researchers become capable of predicting such significant relational fulcrums? First, they discovered that we either bind each other in mutual dysfunction, remain somewhat neutral or mediocre, or free each other into greater health. Then they began to break the mutual dysfunction or function down to its component parts, to the level of behaviors, words, voice tone, facial expression, patterns of action, patterns of inaction, resistances, energies, attitudes, motivations ... the myriad ways people relate to each other. They analyzed the thoughts that drive our words, the motives that shape our facial expressions signifying the interior engine behind our thoughts. Researchers at The Gottman Institute helped open the door to consciousness, to the ways we love or lack love, both subtle and direct.

For the artist, such knowledge is akin to grace.

A fortified, defended, protected, critical, fearful, angry, troubled self inevitably attracts a similarly troubled person. And a self of contentment, peace, discipline, responsibility, community, forgiveness, change, and love attracts like qualities in others. When we gain momentum toward greater wholeness, eventually critical mass is reached and the system surrenders to authentic change: the community, then, has drawn itself into a deeper expression of life. Foresight, a distilled form of personal and collective awareness, leads us to the imaginative capacity to surrender to a deeper sense of our shared humanity. This is not to say perfection is the goal, or attainable. Rather, humility as an understanding of our individual and collective brokenness, becomes the primary posture behind reason, relational health, and love.

In research into human nature, foresight has much to do with a person's facial expressions—researchers at The Gottman Institute started to see certain critical elements in people's faces, like what drove them to become flooded, reactive, and conflictual rather than clear-minded, emotionally discerning or at peace. People's faces showed their reactive emotions, and specific facial expressions became predictors, also revealed in the tone and general wording of the spoken voice and the thoughts driving that voice. How did John Gottman train to achieve such foresight? He went to France and studied for two years under the world's foremost facial expression expert.

His journey to France awakens me as an artist and makes me think, who would we study under regarding artistic foresight? Whose narratives can we find to mentor us in the symmetry of love and power? Shadow and light? Good and evil? I ask myself, how might I surrender to the study of life through the tragedy and uplift these artists carry in their hands? Can I listen fervently enough? Poets like Layli Long Soldier, Natalie Diaz, Claudia Rankine, and so many more provide a place for me to listen.

The gap between conceiving of and bringing something to fullness is wide when we consider the light speed pace of everyday society. Contemplative stability is needed. Quiet wisdom. In the art of Robin Coste Lewis, sable brilliance is powerful, and aligned with or absorbed in the illumination that comes up through darkness, like the light of a candle, or a forest fire at night. Avoiding or denying the reality of either darkness and or light makes art opaque and weakly envisioned. In opening our eyes, in facing ourselves and others with dignity, we see both shadow and light. Deeply-conceived, fiercely-imagined literary art embraces the tension between shadow and light, ingesting it and not running from it. Not fleeing, opposing, ignoring or denying the tension, but seeking to create weighty resolutions that build to a culminating and unifying force.

We know from personal and communal experience, and from scientific study, it takes a long time to change personal character. According to family systems research, it takes a generational family system about fifteen years to move from a living death to fully expressed life together, from the point of total humility, brokenness, and willingness to grow. As a systems psychologist, that's why transitional figures in the generations are so important. Instead of alcoholism, alcoholism, alcoholism, when we find one person who pursues the emotional well-being required not just for sobriety but for depth of life, that person has the capacity to change the generational structure into the future. In organizations and nations, instead of over-ambition, over-dominance, or overuse of power down through the generations, we need a transitional generation: critical density and critical mass, a tipping point into a new and better way of being, where authentic love and authentic power are hand in hand. The Truth and Reconciliation Commission in South Africa, People Power 1 and 2 in the Philippines, the Velvet Revolution in Czechoslovakia, the reconciliation ceremonies of the Nez Perce at the site of the Big Hole Massacre, and the Cheyenne and Arapahoe at the site of the Sand Creek Massacre, the American Civil Rights

Movement—all are examples of a transitional generation reaching critical mass and changing the world.

Similarly, a transitional generation, capable of uncommon foresight, is needed in American literary art. Narrative too weighted toward nihilism lacks love and therefore lacks power, and narrative too weighted toward sentiment lacks power and therefore lacks love. The literary artists who balance love and power today call us back from dissolution and loneliness and lead us to new wellsprings of human connection. The profane and the sacred kiss one another. From these artists we receive value and intimacy, and in their presence we are renewed. In the art of the poem, the short story, the creative nonfiction work, and the novel, the gap in American discernment regarding intimacy shows itself in the undiscerned violence or accruing apathy of men toward women, toward other men, and toward themselves. This is the shadow of which bell hooks and Paulo Freire speak, the age-old patriarchal house of dominance and victimhood in which we all reside regardless of gender, race, or creed. The loss of our mothers and fathers has left us wounded and hungry to enact either hostility or lethargy against ourselves and others. Men in America forfeit their sense of liberatory feminism and so their masculinity is either over-expressed or under-expressed in response to this society-wide epidemic. A blotting out of the feminine results in the fear of intimacy, and the inability to address the spiritual center of life. The art that hails from a deformed sense of masculinity further divides people. Over-expressed or under-expressed masculinity symbolizes the death of relationship and prevents people from coming together on mutually inviting, mutually loving, and mutually powerful terms.

When a man loses or cuts off his sense of liberatory feminism it is as if he has experienced the early death of his mother, a death from which all men find it very difficult to recover.

Similarly, a woman who has a truncated sense of the masculine lives as if she has experienced the premature death of her father, a loss that resounds throughout the lifespan. So the grief we bear is the grief of severe loss. Such death is not only untimely, but psychically and spiritually excruciating. Women in America forfeit their sense of the liberatory masculine and so their feminine ethos is either over-expressed or under-expressed. Hatred for the masculine also results in the fear of intimacy and the erasure of access to a sacred or divine unity. Understanding that personal and biological gender expression, sexual expression, and sexual orientation are natural, complex, and beautiful, the void between the feminine and the masculine (multitudinously defined, as the feminine/masculine dynamic should be) in American art signals the death of the beloved across all gender and sexual dimensions, and it is precisely this alienation between a liberatory feminine and a liberatory masculine that carries pervasive hopelessness in its wake.

Great art, on the other hand, transforms us. A unified feminine/masculine dynamic leads people and nations into greater foresight. This embrace, the feminine for the masculine and the masculine for the feminine, is rarely seen in contemporary American literary art, and speaks to a disintegration at the core of nations. Movements in modernism and early postmodernism, and the styles of fortification men and women crowd themselves with have prevented people and nations from knowing how to love both womanhood and manhood. Contemporary literature overflows with characters characterized by moral malaise, sexual ego, sexual cutoff, or sexual degradation, emotional ego, emotional cutoff, or emotional degradation, grim thinking, crass consciousness and dismal representations of relationship in which discernment (or foresight) and relational intimacy are denied or deemed a fraud. In this sense, art must attend to or pass through the existential emptiness that exists in the present age. How a writer chooses to navigate this passage reveals the writer's vision of humanity.

The notion of an abiding intimacy, championed by bell hooks and many others, suggests something I find to be much more believable than the cynicism, nihilism, and simplistic gnosticism that characterizes much of contemporary Western literature. How much faith does it take to believe life conspires against you and annihilation is existence? I think it takes more faith to convince myself harm and ill will are the only reality than it does to open my eyes to the inviolability of life, the virtue of others, and authentic love. The experience of love, like the experience of a smile, achieves almost immediate affirmation of the existence of a transcendent essence in the world.

From the shadow of the Holocaust in the bowels of a Nazi concentration camp, the Jewish Austrian surgeon and psychiatrist Viktor Frankl had the gall to say this: "The salvation of [humanity] is through love and in love. I understood how a [person] who has nothing left in this world still may know bliss, be it only for a brief moment, in the contemplation of [the] beloved." Frankl also echoed the basic intimacy of our biology when he continued:

Consider the eye. The eye, too, is self-transcendent in a way. The moment it perceives something of itself, its function—to perceive the surrounding world visually—has deteriorated. If it is afflicted with a cataract, it may 'perceive' its own cataract as a cloud; and if it is suffering from glaucoma, it might 'see' its own glaucoma as a rainbow halo around lights. Normally, however, the eye doesn't see anything of itself.

To be human is to strive for something outside of oneself. I use the term "self-transcendence" to describe this quality behind the will to meaning, the grasping for something or someone outside oneself. Like the eye, we are made to turn outward toward another human being to whom we can love and give ourselves.

Only in such a way do people demonstrate themselves to be truly human.

Only when in service of another does a person truly know his or her humanity.

Like Viktor Frankl, Audre Lorde lived in accord with revolutionaries of freedom and those who abandon themselves to love everywhere. She addressed injustices of racism, sexism, classism, heterosexism, and homophobia. Her voice resounds today, the song of a poet who leads us to greater wisdom, health, autonomy, connection, freedom, and communion. Her art unites us in the warm home of her essential understanding and sends us back into the world prepared not only to see more clearly but to love more deeply, not only to challenge but to bring healing. "Pain is important," she said, "how we evade it, how we succumb to it, how we deal with it, how we transcend it. Revolution is not a one-time event."

7.

The Spirit of Life

Breath, Soul, Life

A Quartet

1

On a given weekend not many years ago, Jennifer and I traveled to Montana to see my family. My ugly relationship with my father had transitioned because of his changes and the work we'd done as a family, and now being outdoors together, hunting or fishing, could be treasured again. When Jennifer and I came in the door he kissed me on the cheek. He kissed Jennifer on the cheek.

"Good to see you," he said. "Glad you're safe."

He pulled us in, one at a time.

He is a big man with a big smile and a warm embrace.

"I love you," he said.

2

Psyche in its original definition means *breath, soul, life.*

From this perspective, psychology is very much like art: the medium is the heart and soul of the person. Breath, soul, and life are symbols of the ineffable and we are reminded of this nameless quality when a new child enters the world, when dawn rises, and when spring follows winter. With breath, soul, and life, healing makes things new. For a poet, life is the source of the imagination. Breath. Soul. Life. In this understanding of family and personal identity, psychology is the sister of imagination. Understanding people and history and culture is the difference between art with depth or art plagued by sepsis, between art inbreathed with fire, or art diseased.

Ultimate concerns beget ultimate questions:

What defines human nature?

What is violence?

What is forgiveness?

How does one die well?

How does one wholeheartedly live?

Where does breath come from?

The major theories of psychology are about human nature, how we act and behave, what we believe, and each theory involves various valid and not so valid approaches to why we behave as we do. In a Freudian stance, people are seen as largely determined by sexual and aggressive drives. Behaviorism emphasizes a linear 1-2-3 of how people behave, and if we ascribe to behaviorism's 1-2-3 we may believe we can change our external relational dynamic, and therefore change our way in the world. If we turn to a cognitive-behavioral view, then life is about our thinking, the way we think, and how our thinking works, how our thinking defines how we relate to the world. Finally, around the 1950s systems theory emerged, a way of wisdom I ascribe to in combination with Jungian and existential approaches to life.

In systems psychology each individual is made up of a number of individual elements that in the healthy person form a unified whole. Similarly, all people together are interwoven to form an even greater whole. If we understand the relationship of these elements, we influence both self and others toward more life. If our knowledge is limited or darkened, our influence tends toward fragmentation or disintegration. Of note in foresight from a systems lens, chaos, rot, and deterioration are the nascent preconditions for emergence into a more enriched existence.

Murray Bowen was a systems thought-leader. He said the foundation of health is the person-to-person relationship, the one-to-one relationship with others. The person-to-person relationship is one in which we gather to talk about the relationship without having to digress into speaking about meaningless things or talking about others in a negative light.

Theories of psychology and human nature necessarily entail an appreciation of darkness and how we can better discern and transcend the force of our own darkness. Some theories are clearer than others. In systems theory, the darkness is similar to Jung's conception of the paradoxical relationship of darkness and light that exists in all people. In systems theory, when we are immature we hold others in a dark light instead of admitting our own faults. The immature life is characterized by blame, bitterness, self-avoidance, and lack of healing. This is the typical pattern of people who live frustrated, wounding, or wounded relational lives. A common way for people to self-soothe is to talk about someone else in a degrading way.

Systems psychology, Jungian psychology, and existential psychology all encourage the will to become mature human beings, responsible for the well-being of our families and communities. In the 1950s Bowen, a leading psychiatrist, did things we don't do now. He placed entire families in the hospital for two years at a time. Bowen brought them to the Georgetown Medical Center in Washington D.C., still a major center for Bowenian studies. He studied families because at that time there were no significant inroads regarding healing major mental health problems such as schizophrenia, anorexia, and alcoholism. He saw the family as fertile ground for new discoveries.

Many of the most important research findings in psychology over the last 70 years have their roots in systems psychology. Bowen noticed schizophrenic patients, when hospitalized, often became healthy enough to reintegrate and return to normal functioning through a combination of medication and counseling. But when schizophrenics were released back to society, which meant back to their families, in a matter of weeks the patient would be schizophrenic again. So Bowen started thinking perhaps the family is the issue not the patient. Since the medical model was, and remains, a patriarchal system, the mother was blamed initially. Significantly, such blame of the feminine has a long history not only in psychology but in all fields of human endeavor, as well as in the heart of the family. Bowen and his team came up with one of the strangest names I've ever encountered to describe a psychological disorder: *the schizophrenogenic mother*. Thankfully, further research found the core of the problem was not the mother, and not the schizophrenic patient, but rather what systems thought now refers to as an *identified family* instead of an identified patient, in other words an identified generational system with elements in need of change in order for healing to occur.

In the 1960s Bowen brought families into the hospital for two years at a time to more clearly see what each of the separate members were responsible for in generating illness. Likewise, in the world's finest research about families today at the Gottman Institute in Seattle, the intricate systemic interplay of familial health or dysfunction is laid bare. In the Gottmans' research families are brought in, but only for three days at a time, instead of two years, and they come to an apartment rather than to the hospital. Considering the Gottmans' work in more detail we find, for example, a person who stonewalls—who resists the beloved other and tends to be highly fortified or closed emotionally— is inevitably paired with a person who is consistently critical, and full of contempt for the beloved other. Equally, we find the reverse is also true: one who harbors contempt laced with criticism is inevitably paired with one who stonewalls and is stubbornly defensive. An automatic engine of ill-health bound by unconscious interrelation becomes inevitable. Power is both overt and covert, exerted through dominance and withholding, abuse and victimhood. It can be difficult at times to tell who holds overt power and who holds covert power and how that power is evidenced or enacted. Across gender and sexual orientation, the dominant masculine or feminine, for example, is commonly paired with what appears to be the submissive feminine or masculine. But what this research begins to unfold is that submission most often cloaks hatred, so the inverse of dominance is often hatefulness, a mutual illness-invoking dynamic, as neither dominance nor hatred have succeeded throughout history in accomplishing wholeness, healing, or legitimate reparation, atonement, and reconciliation. Bell hooks refers to this dynamic as the mutually reinforcing patriarchal white supremacist water in which every American is forced to swim, implicating our national genocidal history from slavery, the Native American holocaust, and the pervasive use of force evident from the beginning of America to today. In her conception, a brilliant and unique deepening of some of Paulo Freire's most radiant social philosophies and Greenleaf's poetic leadership approaches, wholeness or healing only arrives individually or collectively through the liberation that rises from authentic love in which humanity humbles itself and willingly loves and serves the highest priority needs of others.

In psychology, as in theology, philosophy, or history we see a balance between that which is determined by what we might call overarching social causal laws, and the mystery or miracle of that which cannot be easily or willfully defined. Quantitative, reductionistic, positivist science tends to seek control by privileging overarching laws, an echo of the patriarchal (dominant and self-enclosed) regime throughout history, whereas qualitative or interpretivist science tends to lean into the mystery, the circular, or a more poststructural approach that often harbors disregard (hatred) for traditional structures. Positivist science is countered by interpretivist science and vice versa. Here in endless recursion something in essence masculine is countered by something in essence feminine and something essentially feminine is countered by something essentially masculine. Not surprisingly, in the scientific comm

unity, wars have been fought between the two camps from the beginnings of "scientific method" until now. Systems theory unites these two polar powers by comprehending their overt and covert expressions, which could be named not only overt and covert disdain but also overt and covert discovery. Because both essences exist within a mutually defined quest for truth, they are in relationship either toward the possibility of ingrained enmity or intrinsic unity.

Jung speaks to this in his mystery-centered blend of feminine and masculine ways of being. By interwoven unity with one another, in the self and in relationship with others, the interpretivist and the reductionist, the mystery and the reason, the qualitative and the quantitative, the female and the male, bring wholeness to life. Some say human nature always ultimately comes down to love and power. Legitimate (healing-oriented) power is often hidden and as it is revealed and made visible, people experience not only less pain but more equity, autonomy, community, and connection. When power and love are enemies, condemned, obscured, denied, abused, or degraded, we experience the world as unjust.

Truly, injustice is a large part of the history of the world, but perhaps not the most powerful or enduring. Again, deaths due to alienation and enmity in the form of war have increased from five million to 20 million to 110 million in the last three centuries. Clearly the world is entrenched in violence, non-love, and anti-love. Yet we also have knowledge of what drives our enmity with each other. The study of the human heart, or individual and collective experience—the study of breath, soul, and life—alters and in fact transforms the individual and the community. When we consider the micro level, we see intimate partnerships, and when we look at holistic loving, we borrow wisdom from Jung, bell hooks, and all who envision humanity whole. In her book *All About Love* hooks states that without love we are not only lonely and alone, but blindly enslaved to the centuries-old harmful regimes alive and well in the world today. And therefore, we enact violence on ourselves and others. On the other hand, when we love, we serve others and gain the opportunity to heal our painful genocidal past.

Imbalance happens between people, in every family, within cultures, in every nation. A balance of legitimate love and power is crucial. Jung leads with gentle clarity. Carl Jung himself was an anomaly, both scientific and delighted with mystery. Considered among the foremost psychologists of the 20th century, his balance of science and mystery is one of the reasons his work does not fall out of fashion. People grow weary of the religion of hard science, and at the same time want something more than the over-subjective bias of simple interpretivism. Jung's theoretical and practical insights enervate interior and communal balance. He presented the notion that everyone is bound by things that stop us from achieving love or being in a secure place in love. Denial, he proposed, is the most common enslavement. Jung also saw denial as the most stubborn and obstinate of human faults. His archetypal images of the hero, the innocent, the explorer, the rebel, the lover, the creator, the holy fool, the sage, the shadow and the light, the masculine and the feminine, the soul, and many other facets of our collective existence were presented as ways of being that life asks us to understand and integrate. Without purposeful integration we tend toward physical, emotional, psychological, and spiritual fracture.

And yet, humanity throughout the globe also embodies the ancient connection between the human and the Divine in which mercy triumphs over justice.

3

One of the most ironic aspects of modernity is that hard science hated, negated, and tried to erase the life of the spirit but became itself one of the most unbending, calcified belief systems the world has ever known. From a Bowenian perspective, or from the perspectives of Virginia Satir in the U.S. or Salvador Minuchin of South America (systems thought-leaders who were Bowen's contemporaries)—any system that is too rigid becomes increasingly vulnerable to fracture. Easily breakable, a rigid system is incapable of gathering to itself the growth impulse needed to take the next steps toward healthy change. To change for the better requires flexibility. Religious systems, pre-dating hard science, have been stricken by the same ever more calcifying dis-ease toward humanity. In a systemic sense, the inverse is also immanently apparent, so when we become either too rigid *or* too open, too severe *or* too loose, the center no longer holds and what once was unity devolves to chaotic infighting riddled with negation, dysfunction, and individual and collective illness, eventuating in greater poverty, marginalization, imprisonment and war.

In the religion of hard science, which is coming into less rigidity and more fluidity to some degree at this point, the only things previously accepted as human were those that could be measured according to the positivist patriarchal regime. In a mirror effect, the super-subjectivity of interpretivism valued deconstruction so highly all became shifting sand in which collective human values were devalued or obliterated. Nihilistic positivist hard science meets the over-expressed relativity of interpretivist understandings at the nadir of human angst and devaluation. Gratefully, in recent years a more developed sense of science has emerged seeking to embrace the linearity, reason and rationality of hard science and the circularity, intimacy, and mystery of qualitative science. Positivism meets interpretivism as coequals in a nonbinary balance of feminine and masculine ways of knowing.

When we return to a well-discerned conception of love we see scientists, women and men, asking questions like, "Wait, are we trying to say that love doesn't exist or compassion doesn't exist because it can't be measured or touched, just as one can't touch or measure forgiveness or gratitude or humor?" At a certain point in the scientific revolution, scientists, almost inalterably blind at the time, boldly declared, "It's true, love does not exist, and neither does God or in fact any intangible human value." But chinks developed in this armor and increasingly in the last 30 or 40 years, scientists throughout the world have succeeded in using the methods of hard science to look at things once considered anathema according to the calcified religion of hard science.

Significantly, in current best practices in social science research, a more bounded, less subjective interpretivist paradigm joins a more open and less inflexible positivist paradigm to create a more unified and *balanced* scientific community. Again, forgiveness is an integral example. A deeper look at forgiveness research speaks to what is possible in social science right now. Using hard science principles with experimental research completely positivist in design, stunning results have come to the fore. To go deeper into a social science truth alluded to earlier, according to scientific scales that measure forgiveness capacity, emotional well-being, and heart trouble, people who have undergone forgiveness-oriented interior work and have attained higher forgiveness capacity tend to also experience significantly lower depression, lower anxiety, lower heart disease, and significantly greater emotional well-being, with bridges being made now on the relationship between stronger forgiveness capacity and stronger immune systems.

From a hard-science perspective, in the scientific literature about forgiveness, a quantitative researcher starts by defining what are called "dimensions." The researcher or research team comes to a somewhat secure set of dimensions based on both the qualitative and quantitative research as shown in the body of literature on forgiveness. In forgiveness, dimensions are those such as the ability to forego the desire to harm someone who has harmed you, the will to forego bitterness, and the will toward peace of mind with regard to the harmful event (a dimension something like grace). Other dimensions can include the ability to notice your own faults previous to noticing the faults of others, pointing toward humility and empathy as powerful components of forgiveness. Science pursues a reductionistic path by "reducing" a topic to its essential dimensions. Questions are then constructed based on the defined dimensions. The questions become a "questionnaire" or "survey instrument" or "scale" given to large groups of people to gather data.

A question such as "How often do you tend to forego anger when you've been harmed?" is then answered on a numbered scale that ranges from "Always" all the way down to "Never." Under normal conditions when social science researchers give out a survey with valid and reliable questions about forgiveness to a few hundred people, a standard bell curve results in which some people score much higher than average, or in social science terms those people score a few standard deviations above the norm and are much higher in their forgiveness capacity, while other people score a few standard deviations below average and are much lower in forgiveness capacity than the majority of the group. The vast majority of people score in the middle of the curve meaning they do not have especially high or low forgiveness capacity. Higher forgiveness capacity is then correlated to scores the group received on different survey instruments designed to measure depression, anxiety, and emotional well-being, as well as physical measures of heart disease and immune system strength. Pair all this with experimental research in which people are led through purposeful interior work to develop their forgiveness capacity, and the before and after effect can be thoroughly tested. The current research in forgiveness is a fascinating blend of circular and linear, qualitative and quantitative discernment. In this sense, the mystery-based intuitive aspects and the more determined aspects of human nature dovetail with one another and achieve a kind of oneness.

The results are as revealing as they are lovely, as powerful as they are enduring.

Currently in hard science, not in the natural sciences but the human sciences, forgiveness, grace, gratitude, and love, as well as other values-based research areas, have begun to be grouped under an umbrella called positive psychological research. This has produced a more crystalline awareness of the darker sides of human nature. We are all familiar with our own denial, the tendency to unconsciously or consciously hide our shadow or the elements of ourselves that define our weaknesses. It becomes obvious who has integrated their shadow and who has not. For example, when a loved one says to you in a fight, "You're really defensive." Most people don't respond by saying, "Thanks for pointing that out. I'd like to work on that."

Except for whom?

Mature people. Mature people are those who respond well.

People who have not integrated their own shadow might respond by saying something like, "I'm not defensive! What the hell are you talking about?"

The hypocrisy is self-evident.

Denial keeps us from the full experience of love.

Similarly, in warlike or peace-making cultures, the differences are self-evident.

Jung himself pointed out that when we deny our faults, we are consumed by shadow. When we are consumed by shadow we project our shadow onto the world with harmful results—we refuse to take responsibility for life and therefore degrade, alienate, and efface others rather than inviting them to help us change and become more whole. To be more whole is to be more capable of honoring the feminine and the masculine in ourselves. For Jung, when we choose denial, instead of living a life of responsible love and appropriate power with others, we fall into blaming our own mediocrity on others, the environment, or God as we perceive God. Jung felt denial (the unwillingness to recognize our faults and change) was humanity's most troublesome fault. But we protect ourselves with good reason, he said, because to look at our own evil head on is to suffer intractable shame and thus to beckon the death of the self. The direct look at our own shadow can be irreducibly traumatic. Therefore, when we are unhealthy we tend to avoid the truth about ourselves at all costs. In order to face the shadow we must do so with great care. Even so, Jung said the way to better ground is a gentle path. To heal our fear of our own shadow, and heal our inability to grow, he said we simply need two things: insight and good will. In the language of family, we need understanding and love. At the crossroads of understanding and love, according to Jung, the human and the Divine intersect.

Jung warns us not to look at the shadow directly. Just give it a sidelong glance, he says, and move slowly by. Then circle back and get a little closer to the shadow. In the end we draw near and finally take our shadow into a loving embrace. The shadow is not unlike night in the wilderness. We have fear. We come to know fear more personally. For Jung, to come face-to-face with the shadow before the soul is prepared takes us to the edge of a dark abyss. From there, we look over and down into the chasm. In the center of that darkness is absolute evil. We know we are capable of such evil, and that look, that brush with absolute evil is self-shattering.

To come face-to-face with the shadow, we need loving partners to shield us and help us take a closer look. This involves the ability to develop or evoke true relationships with others. As we get closer and closer to an integration of the shadow, when someone tells us of our faults, we respond by saying, "Thank you. I appreciate that. I desire to grow and change." We begin to welcome others to tell us our faults.

Art is a good sister, a loyal brother, a loved one who truly loves.

I am thirsty for art that shows full-bodied love.

I believe the territory of breath, soul, and life is found by attending to the shadow, which also keeps us from subduing the light. In this way we do not forego the indispensable truth that there exists in people the seed of atonement. In this world, we suffer. We are burned. We often fall. We sometimes rise. We encounter both love and evil. Do we reach the other side refined or destroyed? This is the defining moment of life and art. The women and men in the most significant narratives of our age face the questions of intimacy faced by us all. Who can console us in the harsh darkness we endure? The shadow of the masculine: violent, severe, and vacuous, meets the light of the feminine: affirming, intimate, inviolable. In like fashion the shadow of the feminine: entangled, cruel, and fearful, meets the light of the masculine: integral, meaningful, powerful.

Regarding the path from life to greater life, from 40 years ago when I was a boy on the reservation to now, a unity exists. Today when I go to a reservation basketball tournament with my dad—and he still plays ball at nearly 80—Native American cultures honor elders and they never fail to honor him. I've found if you invest your life in the people of those small towns and that open land, the returns of friendship, laughter and love are immense. I have hauntings from the reservation that call to me, and hauntings in my own family. I remember those who didn't make it out. My beloved cousin, Jacine. Her long descent into the underground. Her life ripped away in a drug shootout. Blake Walks Nice, knifed to death behind Jimtown Bar. Cleveland Highwalker's suicide. For me, as for others in my family, sorrow is met with sorrow, over my grandfather who died of alcoholism, over our beloved Jacine, and over so many of my boyhood heroes, Native American athletes who died young. Still, I remember the proverb spoken by my wife—many waters cannot quench love, love is stronger than death.

I think of the mountains of Montana, and I think, how is this possible, such grand intimacy in a package that harbors such violence? Wolves kill the young and the old. Bears and mountain lions roam the night. Now consider the person who asks forgiveness and makes atonement even in the face of the most bleak human conditions. Further, consider the fact that if that person's amends-making is true, or if that person's life answers to the demands of reparation, atonement, and reconciliation, through long endurance that one is often welcomed back to community. This occurrence, across people and cultures, the world over, breathes life into the death we know.

Certain themes recur in great art: love and hate, enmity and peace, justice and mercy. Poets engage what they perceive to be God or anti-God, atheism, belief, dogmatics of all forms, the liberation of consciousness, the heights of human history, the abyss of human harm, all the miniscule and expansive ways we live and the core of what gives us gratitude, what breaks us, and what makes us generous, vital, and beautifully dangerous. I find passion in sacred words, sacred affections, friendship, fatherhood, motherhood, sisterhood, brotherhood, devotion, joy, wilderness.

I'm drawn to these because I find the transitory nature of people paired with the infinite or eternal nature of people a braid of radiant splendor. I think we've all been at the trailhead of a path where we acknowledge the need for grace. Yet before we embark on this new terrain we must admit our weaknesses and our need for others. Yes, we fail, and when we fail absolutely the pain is excruciating. Vaclav Havel, the artist and former president of the Czech Republic, wondered if suicides aren't in fact the sad guardians of the meaning of life. Homicides play their own red music largely unknown and undiscerned. As alluded to earlier, in Havel's country, my country of heritage, in protest against the Russian invasion Jan Palach gave his life, twenty years before the Velvet Revolution. To awaken the country from slumber he set himself on fire, burning himself to death in Wenceslas Square in Prague. Our most desperate harms, even those in which our own life has been taken, have latent capacity to awaken us, heal us, and take us deeper into life. For Jan, from the mothers of the Czech lands, and especially from his own mother—we hear the word "miláčku," the Czech word for "darling."

"Art is always transgressive," Makoto Fujimura said. "We need to transgress in love. We have a language to celebrate waywardness. But we do not have a language, a cultural language, to bring people back home." Great art sets us on a journey homeward through the wilderness to gaze once more upon the face of the beloved.

In that gaze, composed of feminine and masculine features, love is revolutionary.

There is a discipline formed of hours and days and years. That devotion, approached through love, carries us and those around us for the rest of our lives. In south central Montana in the heart of the Beartooth Range, night descends. In art as in life we cannot deny the darkness. But at present I don't believe Western art would be accused of denying the darkness but denying the light. Art that humiliates the feminine or the masculine expresses the shattered core of our humanity. In love, peace heals our disintegration.

There are always not only people but words we use flippantly or disgracefully because we haven't discerned our own responsibility to do justice to life. To carry mercy in our hands. For example, one of the most vital words of all healing systems… of any sensible theory of human nature, is the word *listen*. The etymology of "to listen" is "to obey." And many of us in learning that fact would resist or deny or denigrate those origins. But in reality, the etymology is crucial because it speaks to what is most relevant. Eloquent questions become paramount:

What is worthy of our deepest listening? Our deepest obedience?

Our children perhaps. The will to hold life in trust for future generations. The nature of truth in the material and spiritual realms is that we recognize power at the expense of others (or power that abuses) is not legitimate power, while power that heals and gives people more life, freedom, responsibility, and community, is not only legitimate but is the heart of human connection. Through authentic human connection we gain an increased ability to be with one another without violence or greed, contempt or emotional deadness. Family proves this simple truth over and over: genuine love and legitimate power go hand in hand. Love listens. Legitimate power serves. A balance of love and power gives life to others.

4

The night we arrived after the long drive from Spokane to Bozeman, Jennifer and I sat in the kitchen together with my mom and dad and talked until after dark. In the early morning, my father knelt at the side of my bed to wake me. "Time to get up," he said. His voice was soft. He was happy. Now for our journeys into the wilderness he sets out all we need: boots, wool socks, wool pants, gloves, coats, hats, our lunches. He serves. He prepares the breakfast table for us. As we eat together that morning, he reads something from scripture about how a friend loves at all times.

We drive together in the early dark past the Bridger Range and through the gap toward Livingston. We take the turn at Big Timber and head toward the Crazy Mountains just north of the Beartooths. We move quiet over the land, and late in the day he guides me as I shoulder the .243, taking aim. He puts his hands gently on my arms and speaks softly to remind me to hold the rifle level. His voice calms me. I take a breath. In the silence of the valley the shot rings out. We clean and dress the deer in an open field under a wide sky, and we work together, making ready for the return home.

On the way back we stop to eat somewhere, a hamburger shack in another small Montana town. As we enter, he puts his arm around me and says, "I love you. Thanks for being a good son." When he says these words, I am a man and he is my father, and I cry.

Genuine Love

Bell hooks, the dexterous feminist writer and a clarion voice in American life, envisioned a world in which we willingly attune ourselves to the disciplines of love. "Genuine love," she said, "is rarely an emotional space where needs are instantly gratified. To know love we have to invest time and commitment."

In light of her vision, a new understanding rises: people who live well love well, they understand power and become artistic in conversation, they live transparently and develop integrity in response to their own individual and communal faults. In other words, they know and they are known. They lovingly lead others and are led by others, and their relationships are largely free of diminishment. Engagement is infused with a sense of generosity especially in the midst of the fragmentation we so often encounter.

Like hooks, many writers who hail from the wilderness of the American West have influenced me toward deeper love. Consider the rhythmic drive, musicality, and force of Leslie Marmon Silko, the openhanded understanding of Debra Magpie Earling, the sense of witness in the imaginative landscapes of James Welch and N. Scott Momaday. Natalie Diaz and her uncommon truths. Layli Long Soldier's lithe deconstruction of empire. Ruggedness, peace, ferocity, loneliness, and home all become themes in poetry and prose attuned to the reality of love at the foundation of life.

With European philosopher Hans George Gadamer's concept of the eloquent question, we seek to ask of one another questions to which we do not already know the answer. The eloquent question forms a pathway of listening in which we overcome attitudes and behaviors of dominance, negativity, reactivity, fear, anger, or apathy. When we live from darker, more self-absorbed visions we often try to force others to submit to our way of life when their views conflict with our own. But when we live from a more sensible and robust identity we approach those around us as sacred, as *Thou* or *You* in theologian Martin Buber's terms, rather than *It*, as part of the whole creation, the Creator, the Great Mystery. Our conversations and questions result in fulfillment and shared meaning. Initiating and sustaining meaningful dialogue reflects a positive sense of self and others. In art that heals the human heart, writers do this by attending to, honoring, and absorbing the burden of human emptiness. Such artists are adept both at embracing shadow and discerning light.

Dean Ornish, in his decisive work *Love and Survival*, argues (with convincing scientific evidence) that lack of intimacy or lack of emotional and spiritual closeness to others is the root of human illness, and the authentic experience of love is the inner core of what makes us well. Accordingly, the major epidemic of the age is what Ornish calls "emotional and spiritual heart disease, the profound sense of loneliness, isolation, alienation, and depression that are so prevalent today as the social structures that used to provide us with a sense of community and connection break down." Not insignificantly, heart disease is the leading cause of death in America today.

When we consider the children of the nations, we consider the next generation, and the opportunity to forgo self-insulation and give ourselves for the good of others seems almost to cry out to us, calling us to action. The gift of knowing others, and closer still, knowing our own children renews us. With inspiration from my wife and her dynamic life, in the morning I go now to each daughter and touch her face, look into her eyes, and give her a blessing. The words take me into quietness and I come from the blessing better prepared in a human sense, and more grateful. For Natalya, "God has given you the garment of praise instead of the spirit of despair." For Ariana, "God has loved you with an everlasting love. God has drawn you with lovingkindness." For Isabella, "God knows the plans designed for you, plans not for calamity, but for peace. Plans for a future and a hope." Yet even in the echo of a morning ritual that heals me, my own frailty and lack of maturity often stalk me through the day and rear up in my defensiveness, my will to dominate, my lack of patience, my apathy toward even my most valued relationships. Asserting itself in the daily routine of life is my failure to serve the highest priority needs and most holistic desires of the beloved others in my life.

In the wisdom of Freire and hooks, what liberates us is love, an identification with the suffering that always precedes life or growth, and a resolved will to seek that which is necessary to make us whole. This love separates the wheat from the chaff in my life and brings me to my loved ones more vulnerable. I can then gain a place of sanctuary with them in which we find we are capable of living for one another rather than against each other. In this sanctuary joy accompanies us. We move beyond ourselves and see others more clearly. My wife believes mature living is found at the crossroads of imagination and a keenly discerned sense of reality. Emerson referred to this crossroads as the *oversoul,* the place in our collective humanity reserved for humility, wisdom, and generativity:

> ...that Over-soul, within which every [person's] particular being is contained and made one with all others; that common heart, of which all sincere conversation is the worship, to which all right action is submission; that overpowering reality which confutes our tricks and talents, and constrains everyone to pass for what [he or she] is... and which evermore tends to pass into our thought and hand, and become wisdom, and virtue, and power, and beauty. We live in succession, in division, in parts, in particles. Meantime within [humanity] is the soul of the whole; the wise silence; the universal beauty, to which every part and particle is equally related; the eternal ONE.

The Gesture

for Jan Palach, son of the Velvet Revolution

On the surface
he was no exception.

We all cast lots
against the lies of the regime.

Do you agree with the friendly
help of the army? he asked.

We all answered no
and drew straws

until he nodded,
walked to the public square

and lit the match,
his body

made of
light.

The Shadow and the Light

Montana, like a microcosm of the country and the world, is also a staging ground for the most fearsome notions of human love and loss. A proving ground for the question of love in the context of the human and the Divine. Does love exist? Is there sacredness in people and in the natural world? These questions unveil themselves in an America replete with genocidal history, and in a world of genocidal consequence, including the killing sprees of modernity— Hitler and his 23 million murders, Stalin and his 27 million, Mao and his 50 million. No people or country is exempt. America is positioned at the crossroads of her own shadow tendencies and the possibility of a well-seeded ground in which reparations, atonement and forgiveness can take root. The Cheyenne, the Nez Perce, the Lakota, and the Blackfeet, among many sovereign nations, are leading us to new places, as a community of people in beloved relationship.

Forgiveness and atonement are longsuffering, and long in coming.

Touch as a vessel of restoration comes to us from our families, and I wonder at how touch can infuse nations with the will to love. In brutality, the loving touch is turned to its most evil counterpart: violation, rape, erasure, eradication. This ever-present evil, in ourselves and others, requires resolution, an impulse toward transcendence. Such transcendence makes unforeseen demands of us, in our families, our communities, and within and between nations.

In Martin Luther King Jr. and Coretta Scott King's conception of the Beloved Community, "Power without love is reckless and abusive, and love without power is sentimental and anemic. Power at its best is love implementing the demands of justice, and justice at its best is power correcting everything that stands against love. It is precisely this collision of immoral power with powerless morality which constitutes the major crisis of our time. The oppressor will never willingly give up power. By loving the oppressor, we bring about not only our own salvation but the salvation of the oppressor."

MLK also said, "Hate cannot cast out hate. Only love can do that." MLK's wisdom finds affirmation in our hands, our bodies, our touch, when we encounter the grace to give and receive loving touch. My wife used to hold the heel of each of our daughters as they nursed and slept in her arms when they were babies. By loving openly and deeply she showed me that beyond nihilism and our collective shadow, love exists, the sacred exists, and finds expression through touch, emotionally, physically, and spiritually. This touch heals me, and I believe it contains the capacity to bridge our chasms of inhumanity.

Viscerally, in our bodies, we share the anguish of our history.

This makes me question: What can we do with our brutality? How does forgiveness call to us? What atonement can we surrender ourselves to that will lead us back to one another?

Viktor Frankl said there are only two races of people: decent and unprincipled. While this is true, it's also true that reconciling these polarities within our individual and collective life is too complex to fully name, but when it begins to be named in our presence we experience a form of life attuned to our most graceful desires, our most deeply held longings.

The traditional Cheyenne way of leadership, like the traditional Czech way of leadership is honorable: honoring elders and children, women and men. In this context the Divine is also honored. No tribe is perfect, but some ways of being are more mature or more whole than others. The Cheyenne Dog Soldier comes to mind, specifically the dog rope carriers: those who willingly sacrifice their life for the good of the community. In the midst of battle, at the height of its fury, the dog rope carrier slammed a stake in the ground, a stake to which he was tied, signifying, "Here I will fight until I die." Rudolf Otto, in his classic treatise prophetically denouncing fascism in the liminal space between World War I and World War II, referred to God as beyond human discernment. In seeking to gather his thoughts on God he wrote *The Idea of the Holy*, positing the Divine or the numinous as interwoven of three beloved essences he called mysterium tremendum et fascinans. For Otto, as mysterium, the numinous is "wholly other"— entirely different from anything we ordinarily encounter. The numinous evokes a reaction of silence. But the numinous is also mysterium tremendum, provoking terror because it presents itself as overwhelming power. Finally, the numinous is fascinans—merciful, agile, and imbued with love and peace in the wake of cold fate, in the presence of unavoidable suffering, or in the simple observances of everyday life. For Teilhard de Chardin, this was the Divine milieu or the Anima Christi, the soul of Christ, a sacrificial and love-inducing "dynamism of unification" that forms the substrata of all creation, notably taking the feminine form, encompassing the masculine, evolving, ever dying, ever more alive. Atomic and quantum theory, still largely in discovery with regard to the properties of light and the density of gravity present in dark matter, echo Teilhard de Chardin's prophetic vision. Certain though he was, "and ever more certain" that "he must press on in life as though Christ awaited [him] at the term of the universe, at the same time" Teilhard de Chardin felt "no special assurance of the existence of Christ."

"Believing is not seeing," he said. "As much as anyone... I walk in the shadows of faith." As do we all. Once I overheard my young daughter Bella whispering, "the Spirit of the Lord has made me, and the breath of the Almighty gives me life." She turned to me and smiled.

"Hey," I said, "where'd you find those words?"

"They're my favorite now," she said.

I believe the natural world, infused with love, tends toward lyrical beauty even when consumed by terror, trauma, or disaster. "Where were you when I laid the foundations of the earth?" God said to Job, a question as humbling as it is devastating. In Jesuit or Ignatian terms, as desolation follows consolation, consolation follows desolation, a pairing of continual recurrence. On a recent journey flying between England and Spain, two nations, two empires of historical and hateful colonization not unlike the U.S., I reckoned both natural beauty and the history of human evil. John Newton was a slave runner. Lorca was murdered. Washington and Jefferson were slave owners. No one knows precisely what we can do with our own hateful histories, but I think we know there is something to be done, and that something must be done. In the sky above the mighty industrial complexes of London and Barcelona there was bitter blue purity over a bar of white cloud to the far horizon. The obscure, painful, often deadly world is shrouded in the numinous. Our own healthy detachment— not being too swept away by either desolation or consolation—sustains gratitude for life throughout the continuum of our shared and immanent progression from life to death. The Jesuits referred to this as Deus omnia in omnibus, God in all things. The Spanish architect Gaudi said death can never be separated from God. I can't claim to discern the heart of Gaudi's wisdom, but I find the conception beautiful.

The small towns and gigantic landscapes of Montana contain a wealth of intimacy, just as the layered streets of London or Barcelona, Shanghai or São Paulo, New York or L.A. Though it's not for me, I respect a well-formed agnosticism, or a well-discerned atheism. And though I'm not sure what the soul is, it seems to me to be that place from which we seek something deeper and higher than ourselves, something more attuned to the collective affection, wisdom, and vitality we share, informing our daily lives with one another and leading us despite our grave conflicts back to one another. I think the Divine comes to the fore whenever we cross the threshold of grace. Though the question of the existence of God generates a crucible of doubt, I ask for my doubt to be changed. "Lord, heal my unbelief," the ancient text intones. In this hope, I believe in the souls of others even as I embrace the millennia-spanning notion that God desires intimate communion with the soul. And so echoing Emily Dickinson I write words on my heart against impending darkness:

> I am afraid to own a body.
> I am afraid to own a soul.
> Not knowing when the dawn will come, I open every door.

ACKNOWLEDGEMENTS

Some of the essays, poems and interviews in this collection appeared in the following venues, at times in different forms: "Takes Enemy" winner of a Narrative Magazine Silver Prize, and selected by Natalie Diaz for Bodies Built for Game: The Prairie Schooner Anthology of Contemporary Sports Writing; "The Art of Basketball, Writing, and Good Smack Talk: Shann Ray and Jess Walter in Conversation at Tin House" from Tin House online; "Hunger" in Angler's Journal with excerpts from the National Endowment for the Arts Writer's Corner, and the Foreword Readers' Choice Book of the Year Award interview by Hannah Hohman on American Copper for the American Library Association; "After We Lose Our Mothers, What's Left?" selected by Brad Listi for The Nervous Breakdown; "City on the Threshold of Stars" in Blood Fire Vapor Smoke; "Hellroaring Plateau" selected by Chris Dombrowski for Talking River Review; "The Family Who Lived With Their Faces To The Sky" in Balefire, as "3 From Montana" in American Masculine, and as a nonfiction narrative in Forgiveness and Power in the Age of Atrocity; "My Dad, in America" selected by Christian Wiman for Poetry magazine, and in Balefire; "Hesperus" selected by Christian Wiman for Poetry magazine, and in Sweetclover; "Mountain Men," selected by Joe Wilkins for High Desert Journal; "Going to the Sun Road" selected by Greg Michaelson for LitHub; "Eros and Logos" began as part of an interview by Shawn Vestal for The Barking; "On Violence and Faith," from an interview with Brad Listi, Jonathan Evison, and Gloria, LLZ, and EOL at The Nervous Breakdown; "Breath, Soul, Life," from an interview on KPBX, Spokane NPR affiliate; "The Shadow and the Light," from an interview by Peter Geye in Fiction Writers Review; and "The Gesture" in Balefire. To the editors at these venues, my gratitude, and to Aquinas, Augustine, and Paul Lisicky for the axiom: to name God is to be separate from God.

ABOUT THE AUTHOR

American Book Award winner Shann Ray is the author of the poetry collections *Atomic Theory 7*, *Sweetclover*, and *Balefire*. He is also the author of the short story collections *Blood Fire Vapor Smoke*, and *American Masculine*, the novel *American Copper*, the libretto *The Garment of Praise*, and a book of political theory *Forgiveness and Power in the Age of Atrocity*. Ray's work has been featured in *Poetry*, *Esquire*, *McSweeney's*, *Montana Quarterly*, *Big Sky Journal*, *Poetry International*, *Narrative*, *Prairie Schooner*, and *Salon*. Ray spent part of his childhood on the Northern Cheyenne reservation in southeast Montana and has served as a scholar of leadership and forgiveness studies in Africa, Asia, Europe, and the Americas. A former Bread Loaf and NEA fellow, other awards include the High Plains Book Award for poetry and fiction, the Western Writers of America Spur Award, the Poetry Quarterly Prize, and the Foreword Book of the Year Readers' Choice Award. A clinical psychologist specializing in the psychology of men, Ray lives with his wife and daughters in Spokane, Washington, and teaches at Gonzaga University.

ABOUT THE PRESS

Unsolicited Press is a small publisher with a strong focus on poetry, fiction, and creative nonfiction that seeks to push the limits of literature. Some authors the team has worked with include John W. Bateman, Amy Shimshon-Santo, Taylor Garcia, and Kadzi Mutizwa.

Learn more at unsolicitedpress.com

Find the press on twitter and instagram: @unsolicitedp

CPSIA information can be obtained
at www.ICGtesting.com
Printed in the USA
LVHW011602270122
709432LV00004B/254